Providence Brown & Sharpe manufacturing co.

Practical Treatise on Gearing

Fifth Edition

Providence Brown & Sharpe manufacturing co.

Practical Treatise on Gearing
Fifth Edition

ISBN/EAN: 9783337106348

Printed in Europe, USA, Canada, Australia, Japan

Cover: Foto ©ninafisch / pixelio.de

More available books at **www.hansebooks.com**

ON

GEARING.

FIFTH EDITION.

PROVIDENCE, R. I.
BROWN & SHARPE MANUFACTURING COMPANY.

1896.

Entered according to Act of Congress, in the year 1896 by
BROWN & SHARPE MFG. CO.,
In the Office of the Librarian of Congress at Washington.
Registered at Stationers' Hall, London, Eng.
All rights reserved.

PREFACE.

This Book is made for men in practical life; for those who would like to know how to construct gear wheels, but whose duties do not afford them sufficient leasure for acquiring a technical knowledge of the subject.

CONTENTS.

PART I.

CHAPTER I.
Pitch Circle—Pitch—Tooth—Space—Addendum or Face—
Flank—Clearance.................................... 1

CHAPTER II.
Classification—Sizing Blanks and Tooth Parts from Circular
Pitch—Center Distance............................ 5

CHAPTER III.
Single Curve Gears of 30 Teeth and over................. 9

CHAPTER IV.
Rack to Mesh with Single Curve Gears having 30 Teeth and
over... 12

CHAPTER V.
Diametral Pitch—Sizing Blanks and Teeth—Distance between
Centers of Wheels................................ 16

CHAPTER VI.
Single-Curve Gears, having Less than 30 Teeth—Gears and
Racks to Mesh with Gears having Less than 30 Teeth... 20

CHAPTER VII.
Double-Curve Teeth—Gear of 15 Teeth—Rack............. 25

CHAPTER VIII.
Double-Curve Gears, having More and Less than 15 Teeth—
Annular Gears.................................... 30

CHAPTER IX.
Bevel Gear Blanks..................................... 34

CHAPTER X.
Bevel Gears—Form and Size of Teeth—Cutting Teeth...... 41

CHAPTER XI.

Worm Wheels—Sizing Blanks of 32 Teeth and over.......... 62

CHAPTER XII.

Sizing Gears when the Distance between Centers and the Ratio of Speeds are fixed—General Remarks—Width of Face of Spur Gears—Speed of Gear Cutters—Table of Tooth Parts... 77

PART II.

CHAPTER I.

Tangent of Arc and Angle................ 91

CHAPTER II.

Sine, Cosine and Secant—Some of their Applications in Macnine Construction.............................. 97

CHAPTER III.

Application of Circulur Functions—Whole Diameter of Bevel Gear Blanks—Angles of Bevel Gear Blanks.................... 106

CHAPTER IV

Spiral Gears—Calculations for Pitch of Spirals............. 113

CHAPTER V.

Examples in Calculations of Pitch of Spirals — Angle of Spiral—Circumference of Spiral Gears—A few Hints on Cutting 117

CHAPTER VI.

Normal Pitch of Spiral Gears—Curvature of Pitch Surface—Formation of Cutters............................ ... 122

Chapter VII.
Screw Gears and Spiral Gears—General Remarks 128

Chapter VIII.
Continued Fractions—Some Applications in Machine Construction. 130

Chapter IX.
Angle of Pressure................................. 137

Chapter X.
Internal Gears—Tables—Index..................... 139

Chapter XI.
Strength of Gears—Tables 142

PART I.

CHAPTER I.

PITCH CIRCLE, PITCH, TOOTH, SPACE, ADDENDUM OR FACE, FLANK, CLEARANCE.

Let two cylinders, Fig. 1, touch each other, their axes be parallel and the cylinders be on shafts, turning freely. If, now, we turn one cylinder, the adhesion of its surface to the surface of the other cylinder will make that turn also. The surfaces touching each other, without slipping one upon the other, will evidently move through the same distance in a given time. This surface speed is called *linear velocity*.

<small>Original Cylinders.</small>

<small>Linear Velocity.</small>

TANGENT CYLINDERS.

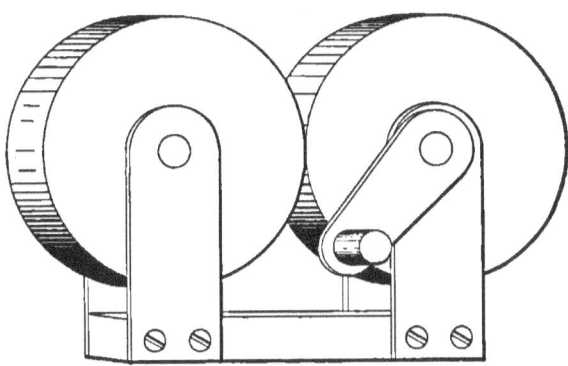

Fig. 1

LINEAR VELOCITY is the distance a point moves along a line in a unit of time.

The line described by a point in the circumference of either one of these cylinders, as it rotates, may be called an arc. The length of the arc (which may be greater or less than the circumference of cylinder), described in a unit of time, is the velocity. The length, expressed in linear units, as inches, feet, etc., is the linear velocity.

The length, expressed in angular units, as degrees, is the **angular velocity**.

Angular Velocity. If now, instead of 1° we take 360°, or one turn, as the angular unit, and 1 minute as the time unit, the angular velocity will be expressed in turns or revolutions per minute.

Relative Angular Velocity. If these two cylinders are of the same size, one will make the same number of turns in a minute that the other makes. If one cylinder is twice as large as the other, the smaller will make two turns while the larger makes one, but the linear velocity of the surface of each cylinder remains the same.

This combination would be very useful in mechanism if we could be sure that one cylinder would always turn the other without slipping.

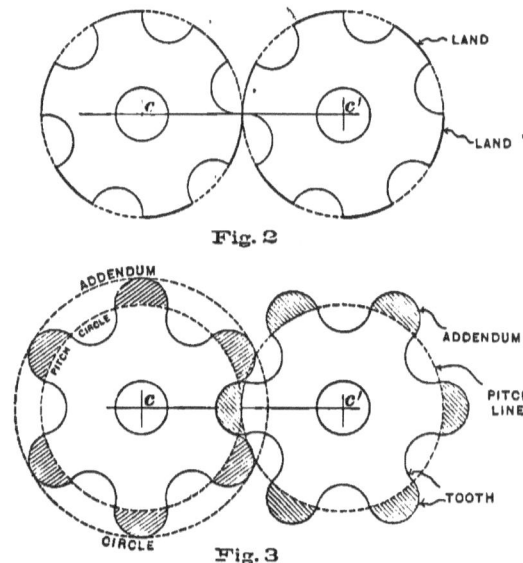

Fig. 2

Fig. 3

Land.
Addendum.
Tooth.
Gear.
Train.

In the periphery of these two cylinders, as in Fig. 2, cut equidistant grooves. In any grooved piece the places between grooves are called *lands*. Upon the lands add parts; these parts are called addenda. A land and its addendum is called a *tooth*. A toothed cylinder is called a *gear*. Two or more gears with teeth interlocking are called a *train*. A line, $c\ c'$, Fig.

2 or 3, between the centers of two wheels is called the *line of centers*. A circle just touching the addenda is called the *addendum circle*.

Line of Centers.
Addendum Circle.

The circumference of the cylinders without teeth is called the *pitch circle*. This circle exists geometrically in every gear and is still called the pitch circle or the primitive circle. In the study of gear wheels, it is the problem to so shape the teeth that the pitch circles will just touch each other without slipping.

Pitch Circle.
Pitch Circle is also called the Primitive Circle.

On two fixed centers there can turn only two circles, one circle on each center, in a given relative angular velocity and touch each other without slipping.

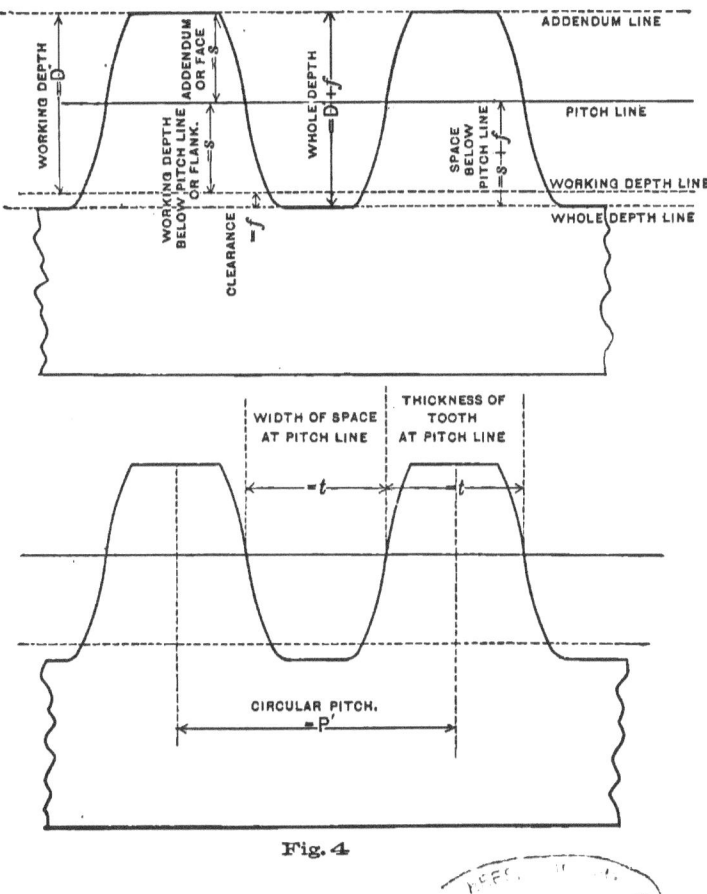

Fig. 4.

Space. The groove between two teeth is called a *space*. In cut gears the width of space at pitch line and thickness of tooth at pitch line are equal. The distance between the center of one tooth and the center of the **Circular Pitch.** next tooth, measured along the pitch line, is the *circular pitch;* that is, the circular pitch is equal to a **Tooth Thickness.** tooth and a space; hence, the thickness of a tooth at the pitch line is equal to one-half the circular pitch.

Abbreviations of Parts for Teeth and Gear.

Let D = diameter of addendum circle.
" D' = " " pitch "
" P' = circular pitch.
" t = thickness of tooth at pitch line.
" s = addendum or face, also length of working part of tooth below pitch line or flank.
" $2s = D''$ or twice the addendum, equals the working depth of teeth of two gears in mesh.
" f = clearance or extra depth of space below working depth.
" $s + f$ = depth of space below pitch line.
" $D'' + f$ = whole depth of space.
" N = number of teeth in one gear.
" π = 3.1416 or the circumference when diameter is 1.

P' is read "P prime." D'' is read "D second." π is read, "pi."

To find the Circumference and Diameter of a Circle. If we multiply the diameter of any circle by π, the product will be the circumference of this circle. If we divide the circumference of any circle by π, the quotient will be the diameter of this circle.

CHAPTER II.

CLASSIFICATION—SIZING BLANKS AND TOOTH PARTS FROM CIRCULAR PITCH—CENTRE DISTANCE—PATTERN GEARS.

If we conceive the pitch of a pair of gears to be made the smallest possible, we ultimately come to the conception of teeth that are merely lines upon the original pitch surfaces. These lines are called *elements* of the teeth. Gears may be classified with reference to the elements of their teeth, and also with reference to the relative position of their axes or shafts. In most gears the elements of teeth are either straight lines or helices (screw-like lines). Elements of the Teeth.

In PART I. of this work, we shall treat upon THREE KINDS OF GEARS:

First—SPUR GEARS; those connecting parallel shafts and whose tooth elements are straight. Spur Gears.

Second—BEVEL GEARS; those connecting shafts whose axes meet when sufficiently prolonged, and the elements of whose teeth are straight lines. In bevel gears the surfaces that touch each other, without slipping, are upon cones or parts of cones whose apexes are at the same point where axes of shafts meet. Bevel Gears.

Third—SCREW OR WORM GEARS; those connecting shafts that are neither parallel nor meet, and the elements of whose teeth are helical or screw-like. Screw or Worm Gears.

The circular pitch and number of teeth in a wheel being given, the diameter of the wheel and size of tooth parts are found as follows: Sizing Blanks, &c.

Dividing by 3.1416 is the same as multiplying by $\frac{1}{3.1416}$. Now $\frac{1}{3.1416} = .3183$; hence, multiply the circumference of a circle by .3183 and the product will be the diameter of the circle. Multiply the circular pitch by .3183 and the product will be the same *part* of the diameter of pitch circle that the circular pitch is of the circumference of pitch circle. This part or *modulus* is called *a diameter pitch*. There are as many diameter pitches contained in the diameter of pitch circle as there are teeth in the wheel.

A Diameter Pitch.

Most mechanics make the addendum of teeth equal to one diameter pitch. Hence we can designate this modulus or diameter pitch by the same letter as we do the addendum; that is, let $s =$ a diameter pitch.

A Diameter Pitch and the Addendum measure the same, radially.

$.3183 \ P' = s$, or circular pitch multiplied by $.3183 = s$, or a diameter pitch.

$Ns = D'$, or number of teeth in a wheel, multiplied by a diameter pitch, equals diameter of pitch circle.

Diameter of Pitch Circle.

$(N + 2) \ s = D$, or add 2 to the number of teeth, multiply the sum by s and product will be the whole diameter.

Whole Diameter.

$\frac{t}{10} = f$, or one tenth of thickness of tooth at pitch-line equals amount added to bottom of space for clearance.

Clearance.

Some mechanics prefer to make f equal to $\frac{1}{16}$ of the working depth of teeth, or $.0625 \ D''$. One-tenth of the thickness of tooth at pitch-line is more than one-sixteenth of working depth, being $.07854 \ D''$.

Example.

Example.—Wheel 30 teeth, $1\frac{1}{2}''$ circular pitch. $P' = 1.5''$; then $t = .75''$ or thickness of tooth equals $\frac{3}{4}''$. $s = 1.5'' \times .3183 = .4775'' =$ a diameter pitch. (See tables of tooth parts, pages 68–71).

Sizes of Blank and Tooth Parts for Gear of 30 teeth, 1½ in. circular pitch.

$D' = 30 \times .4775'' = 14.325'' =$ diameter of pitch-circle.

$D = (30 + 2) \times .4775'' = 15.280'' =$ diameter of addendum circle.

$f = \frac{1}{10}$ of $.75'' = .075'' =$ clearance at bottom of space.

$D'' = 2 \times .4775'' = .9549'' =$ working depth of teeth.

$D'' + f = 2 \times .4775'' + .075'' = 1.0299'' =$ whole depth of space.

$s + f = .4775'' + .075'' = .5525'' =$ depth of space inside of pitch-line.

$D'' = 2s$ or the working depth of teeth is equal to two diameter pitches.

In making calculations it is well to retain the fourth place in the decimals, but when drawings are passed into the workshop, three places of decimals are sufficient.

PROVIDENCE, R. I.

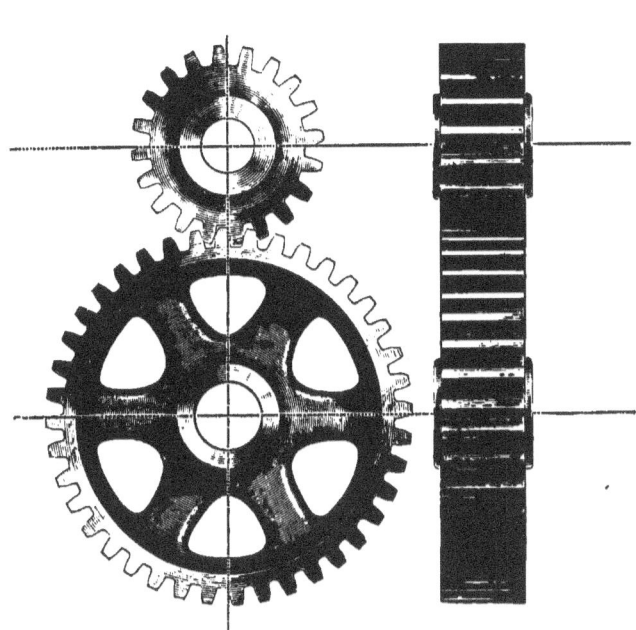

FIG. 5, SPUR GEARING.

Distance between centers of two Gears. The distance between the centers of two wheels is evidently equal to the radius of pitch-circle of one wheel added to that of the other. The radius of pitch-circle is equal to s multiplied by one-half the number of teeth in the wheel.

Hence, if we know the number of teeth in two wheels, in mesh, and the circular pitch, to obtain the distance between centers we first find s; then multiply s by one-half the sum of number of teeth in both wheels and the product will be distance between centers.

Example —What is the distance between the centers of two wheels 35 and 60 teeth, $1\frac{1}{4}''$ circular pitch. We first find s to be $1\frac{1}{4}'' \times .3183 = .3979''$. Multiplying by 47.5 (one-half the sum of 35 and 60 teeth) we obtain 18.899'' as the distance between centers.

Allowance for Shrinkage in Gear Castings. **Pattern Gears** should be made large enough to allow for shrinkage in casting. In cast-iron the shrinkage is about $\frac{1}{8}$ inch in one foot. For gears one to two feet in diameter it is well enough to add simply $\frac{1}{100}$ of diameter of finished gear to the pattern. In gears about six inches diameter or less, the moulder will generally rap the pattern in the sand enough to make any allowance for shrinkage unnecessary. In pattern gears the spaces between teeth should be cut wider than finished gear spaces to allow for rapping and to avoid having too much cleaning to do in order to have gears run freely. In cut patterns of iron it is generally

Metal Pattern Gears. enough to make spaces .015'' to .02'' wider. This makes clearance .03'' to .04'' in the patterns. Some moulders might want .06'' to .07'' clearance.

Metal patterns should be cut straight; they work better with no draft. It is well to leave about .005'' to be finished from side of patterns after teeth are cut; this extra stock to be taken away from side where cutter comes through so as to take out places where stock is broken out. The finishing should be done with file or emery wheel, as turning in a lathe is likely to break out stock as badly as a cutter might do.

If cutters are kept sharp and care is taken when coming through the allowance for finishing is not necessary and the blanks may be finished before they are cut.

CHAPTER III.
SINGLE-CURVE GEARS OF 30 TEETH AND OVER.

Single-curve teeth are so called because they have but one curve by theory, this curve forming both face and flank of tooth sides. In any gear of thirty teeth and more, this curve can be a single arc of a circle whose radius is one-fourth the radius of the pitch circle. In gears of thirty teeth and more, a fillet is added at bottom of tooth, to make it stronger, equal in radius to one-sixth the widest part of tooth space. *Single Curve Teeth.*

A cutter formed to leave this fillet has the advantage of wearing longer than it would if brought up to a corner.

In gears less than thirty teeth this fillet is made the same as just given, and sides of teeth are formed with more than one arc, as will be shown in Chapter VI.

Having calculated the data of a gear of 30 teeth, $\frac{3}{4}$ inch circular pitch (as we did in Chapter II. for $1\frac{1}{2}'' = \frac{3}{4}''$ pitch), we proceed as follows: *Example of a Gear, N=30, P' $=\frac{3}{4}''$.*

1. Draw pitch circle and point it off into parts equal to one-half the circular pitch. *Geometrical Construction. Fig. 6.*

2. From one of these points, as at B, Fig. 6, draw radius to pitch circle, and upon this radius describe a semicircle; the diameter of this semicircle being equal to radius of pitch circle. Draw addendum, working depth and whole depth circles.

3. From the point B, Fig. 6, where semicircle, pitch circle and outer end of radius to pitch circle meet, lay off a distance upon semicircle equal to one-fourth the radius of pitch circle, shown in the figure at BA, and is laid off as a chord.

4. Through this new point at A, upon the semicircle, draw a circle concentric to pitch circle. This last is

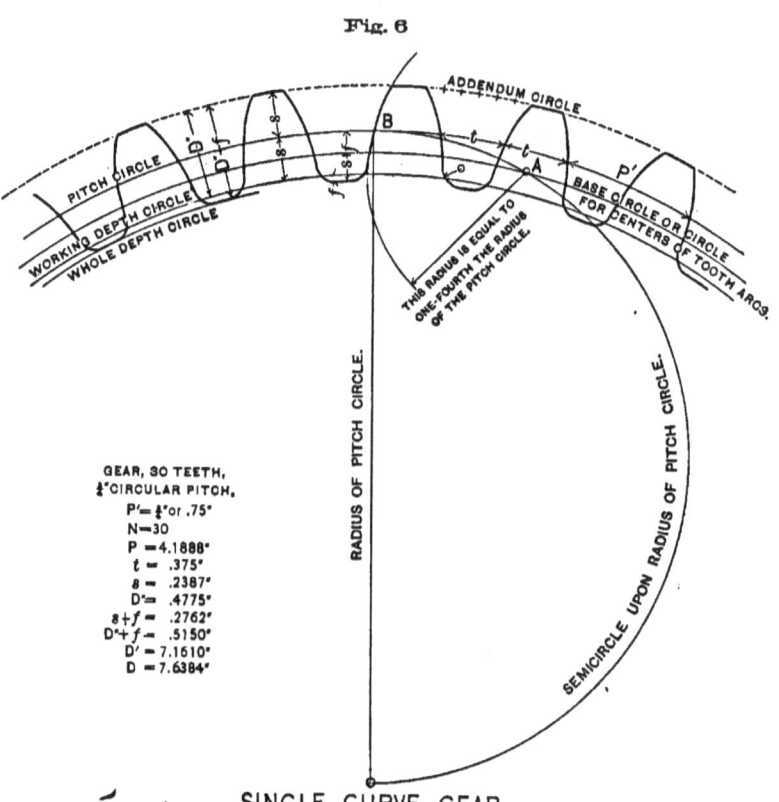

Fig. 6

SINGLE CURVE GEAR.

GEAR, 30 TEETH,
¾" CIRCULAR PITCH.
P'= ¾" or .75"
N=30
P = 4.1888"
t = .375"
s = .2387"
D'= .4775"
s+f = .2762"
D'+f = .5150"
D' = 7.1610"
D = 7.6384"

called the *base circle*, and is the one for centers of tooth arcs. In the system of single curve gears, we have adopted the diameter of this circle is .968 of the diameter of pitch circle. Thus the base circle of any gear 1 inch pitch diameter by this system is .968". If the pitch circle is 2" the base circle will be 1.936."

5. With dividers set to one-quarter of the radius of pitch circle, draw arcs forming sides of teeth, placing one leg of the dividers in the base circle and letting the other leg describe an arc through a point in the pitch circle that was made in laying off the parts equal to one-half the circular pitch. Thus an arc is drawn about A as center through B.

6. With dividers set to one-sixth of the widest part of tooth space, draw the fillets for strengthening teeth at their roots. These fillet arcs should just touch the whole depth circle and the sides of teeth already described.

Single curve or involute gears are the *only* gears that can run at varying distance of axes and transmit unvarying angular velocity. This peculiarity makes involute gears specially valuable for driving rolls or any rotating pieces, the distance of whose axes is likely to be changed.   *Peculiarity of Involute Gearing.*

The assertion that gears crowd harder on bearings when of involute than when of other forms of teeth, has not been proved in actual practice.   *Pressure on bearings.*

Before taking next chapter, the learner should make several drawings of gears 30 teeth and more. Say make 35 and 70 teeth $1\frac{1}{4}$" P'. Then make 40 and 65 teeth $\frac{7}{8}$" P'.   *Practice, before taking next chapter.*

An excellent practice will be to make drawing on cardboard or Bristol-board and cut teeth to lines, thus making paper gears; or, what is still better, make them of sheet metal. By placing these in mesh the learner can test the accuracy of his work.

CHAPTER IV.

RACK TO MESH WITH SINGLE-CURVE GEARS HAVING 30 TEETH AND OVER.

Diagram, made preparatory to drawing a Rack. This gear (Fig. 7) is made precisely the same as gear in Chapter III. It makes no difference in which direction the construction radius is drawn, so far as obtaining form of teeth and making gear are concerned.

Here the radius is drawn perpendicular to pitch line of rack and through one of the tooth sides, B. A semicircle is drawn on each side of the radius of the pitch circle.

The points A and A' are each distant from the point B, equal to one-fourth the radius of pitch circle and correspond to the point A in Fig. 6.

In Fig. 7 add two lines, one passing through B and A and one through B and A'. These two lines form angles of $75\frac{1}{2}°$ (degrees) with radius BO. Lines BA and BA' are called lines of pressure. The sides of rack teeth are made perpendicular to these lines.

Rack. A **Rack** is a straight piece, having teeth to mesh with a gear. A rack may be considered as a gear of infinitely long radius. The circumference of a circle approaches a straight line as the radius increases, and when the radius is infinitely long any finite part of the circumference is a straight line. The pitch line of a rack, then, is merely a straight line just touching the pitch circle of a gear meshing with the rack. The thickness of teeth, addendum and depth of teeth below pitch line are calculated the same as for a wheel. (For pitches in common use, see table of tooth parts.)

Construction of Pitch Line of Rack.

The term *circular pitch* when applied to racks can be more accurately replaced by the term *linear pitch* Linear applies strictly to a line in general while circular pertains to a circle. Linear pitch means the distance between the centres of two teeth on the pitch line whether the line is straight or curved.

A rack to mesh with a single-curve gear of 30 teeth or more is drawn as follows:

1. Draw straight pitch line of rack; also draw addendum line, working depth line and whole depth line, each parallel to the pitch line (see Fig. 7).

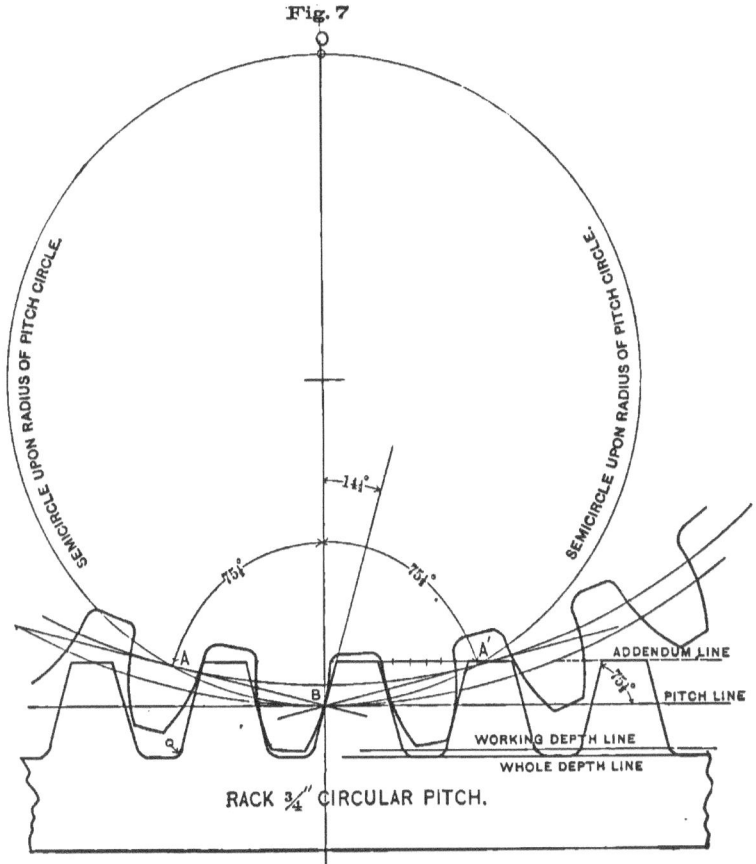

Rack.
Fig. 7.

RACK TO MESH WITH SINGLE CURVE GEAR
HAVING 30 TEETH AND OVER.

2. Point off the pitch line into parts equal to one-half the circular pitch, or $= t$.

3. Through these points draw lines at an angle of $75\tfrac{1}{2}°$ with pitch lines, alternate lines slanting in opposite directions. The left-hand side of each rack tooth is perpendicular to the line BA. The right-hand side of each rack tooth is perpendicular to the line BA'.

4. Add fillets at bottom of teeth equal to $\tfrac{1}{5}$ of the width of spaces between the rack teeth at the addendum line.

Angle for sides of Rack Teeth. The sketch, Fig. 8, will show how to obtain angle of sides of rack teeth, directly from pitch line of rack, without drawing a gear in mesh with the rack.

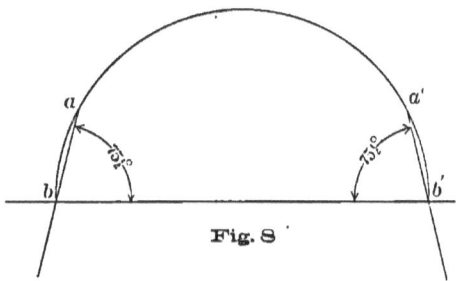

Fig. 8

Upon the pitch line $b\ b'$, draw any semicircle— $b\ a\ a'\ b'$. From point b lay off upon the semicircle the distance $b\ a$, equal to one-quarter of the diameter of semicircle, and draw a straight line through b and a.

This line, $b\ a$, makes an angle of $75\tfrac{1}{2}°$ with pitch line $b\ b'$, and can be one side of rack tooth. The same construction, $b'\ a'$, will give the inclination $75\tfrac{1}{2}°$ in the opposite direction for the other side of tooth.

The sketch, Fig. 9, gives the angle of sides of a tool for planing out spaces between rack teeth. Upon any line OB draw circle OABA'. From B lay off distance BA and BA', each equal to one-quarter of diameter of the circle.

Draw lines OA and OA'. These two lines form an angle of 29°, and are right for inclination of sides of rack tool.

Make end of rack tool .31 of circular pitch, and then round the corners of the tool to leave fillets at the bottom of rack teeth. Width of Rack Tool at end.

Thus, if the circular pitch of a rack is 1½" and we multiply by .31, the product .465" will be the width of tool at end for rack of this pitch before corners are taken off. This width is shown at *x y*.

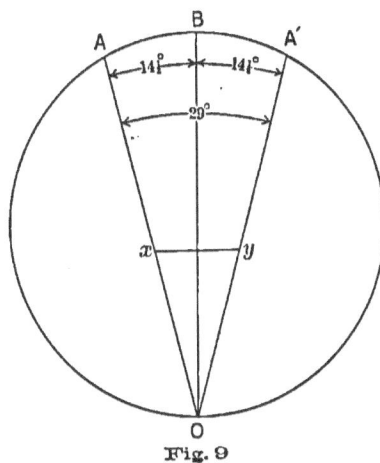

Fig. 9

This sketch and the foregoing rule are also right for a worm-thread tool, but a worm-thread tool is not usually rounded for fillet. In cutting worms, leave width of top of thread .335 of the circular pitch. When this is done, the depth of thread will be right. Worm Thread Tool.

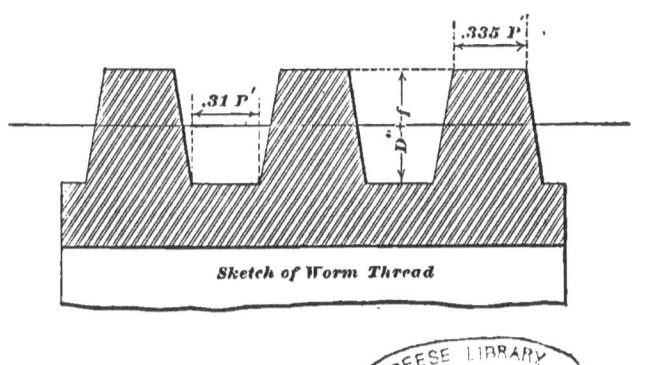

Sketch of Worm Thread

CHAPTER V.

DIAMETRAL PITCH—SIZING BLANKS AND TEETH—DISTANCE BETWEEN CENTRES OF WHEELS.

<small>When it is necessary to know the Circular Pitch.</small> In making drawings of gears, and in cutting racks, it is necessary to know the circular pitch, both on account of spacing teeth and calculating their strength. It would be more convenient to express the circular pitch in whole inches, and the most natural divisions <small>In a complete Wheel, the Pitch Circumference must contain the Circular Pitch, some whole number of times.</small> of an inch, as $1''$ P', $\frac{3}{4}''$ P', $\frac{1}{2}''$ P', and so on. But as the circumference of the pitch circle must contain the circular pitch some whole number of times, corresponding to the number of teeth in the gear, the diameter of the pitch circle will often be of a size not readily measured with a common rule. This is because the circumference of a circle is equal to 3.1416 times the diameter, or the diameter is equal to the circumference multiplied by .3183.

In practice, it is better that the diameter should be <small>Pitch, in Terms of the Diameter.</small> of some size conveniently measured. The same applies to the distance between centers. Hence it is generally more convenient to assume the pitch in terms of the diameter. In Chapter II. was given a definition of a diameter pitch, and also how to get a diameter pitch from the circular pitch.

We can also assume a diameter pitch and pass to its <small>Circular Pitch and a Diameter Pitch.</small> equivalent circular pitch. If the circumference of the pitch circle is divided by the number of teeth in the gear, the quotient will be the circular pitch. In the same manner, if the *diameter* of the pitch circle is divided by the number of teeth, the quotient will be a diameter pitch. Thus, if a gear is 12 inches pitch diameter and has 48 teeth, dividing $12''$ by 48, the quotient $\frac{1}{4}''$ is a diameter pitch of this gear. In practice, a diameter pitch is taken in some convenient part of an inch, as $\frac{1}{2}''$ diameter pitch, and so on. It is convenient in calculation to designate one of these diameter pitches by s, as in Chapter II. Thus, for $\frac{1}{4}''$ diameter pitch, s is equal to $\frac{1}{4}''$. Generally, in speaking of diameter pitch, the denominator of the fraction only is named. $\frac{1}{8}''$ diameter pitch is then called 8 *diametral pitch*. That is, it has been found more convenient to take the *reciprocal* of a diameter pitch in making calculation. The reciprocal of a number is 1, divided by that number. Thus the reciprocal of $\frac{1}{4}$ is 4, because $\frac{1}{4}$ goes into 1 four times. Abbreviation of Diameter Pitch. Reciprocal of a Number.

Hence, we come to the common definition:

DIAMETRAL PITCH is the number of teeth to *one inch* of diameter of pitch circle. Let this be denoted by P. Thus, $\frac{1}{4}''$ diameter pitch we would call 4 *diametral pitch* or 4 P, because there would be 4 teeth to every inch in the diameter of pitch circle. The circular pitch and the different parts of the teeth are derived from the diametral pitch as follows. Diametral Pitch.

$\frac{3.1416}{P} = P'$, or 3.1416 divided by the diametral pitch is equal to the circular pitch. Thus to obtain the circular for 4 diametral pitch, we divide 3.1416 by 4 and get .7854 for the circular pitch, corresponding to 4 diametral pitch. Given, the Diametral to find the Circular Pitch. To obtain Circular Pitch from Diametral Pitch.

In this case we would write P=4, P'=.7854'', $s=\frac{1}{4}''$.

$\frac{1}{P}''=s$, or one inch divided by the number of teeth to an inch, gives distance on diameter of pitch circle occupied by *one* tooth. The addendum or face of tooth is the same distance as s.

$\frac{1}{s}=P$, or one inch divided by the distance occupied by one tooth equals number of teeth to one inch.

$\frac{1.57}{P}=t$, or 1.57 divided by the diametral pitch gives thickness of tooth at pitch line. Thus, thickness of teeth along the pitch line for 4 diametral pitch is .392''. Given, the Diametral Pitch to find the Thickness of Tooth at the Pitch Line.

$\frac{N}{P}=D'$, or number of teeth in a gear divided by the diametral pitch equals diameter of the pitch circle. Thus for a wheel, 60 teeth, 12 P, the diameter of pitch circle will be 5 inches. Given, the Number of Teeth in a wheel and the Diametral Pitch to find the Diameter of Pitch Circle.

$\frac{N+2}{P}=D$, or add 2 to the number of teeth in a wheel and divide the sum by the diametral pitch, and the Given, the Number of Teeth in a wheel and the Diametral Pitch to find the Whole Diameter.

quotient will be the *whole diameter* of the gear or the diameter of the addendum circle. Thus, for 60 teeth, 12 P, the diameter of gear blank will be $5\frac{2}{12}$ inches.

$\frac{N}{D'}=P$, or number of teeth divided by diameter of pitch circle in inches, gives the diametral pitch or number of teeth to one inch. Thus, in a wheel, 24 teeth, 3 inches pitch diameter, the diametral pitch is 8.

$\frac{N+2}{D}=P$, or add 2 to the number of teeth; divide the sum by the whole diameter of gear, and the quotient will be the diametral pitch. Thus, for a wheel $3\frac{2}{10}''$ diameter, 14 teeth, the diametral pitch is 5.

$P D'=N$, or diameter of pitch circle, multiplied by diametral pitch equals number of teeth in the gear. Thus, in a gear, 5 pitch, 8'' pitch diameter, the number of teeth is 40.

$\frac{D}{N\times 2}=s$, or divide the whole diameter of a spur gear by the number of teeth plus two, and the quotient will be the addendum, or a diameter pitch.

A Diameter Pitch. In future, when we speak of *a diameter pitch*, we shall mean the addendum distance or s. If we speak of so many diameter pitches, we shall mean so many *The Diametral Pitch.* times s, ($\frac{1''}{P}=s$). When we say *the diametral pitch* we shall mean the number of teeth to one inch of diameter of pitch circle, or P, ($\frac{1''}{s}=P$).

To obtain Diametral Pitch from Circular Pitch. When the circular pitch is given, to find the corresponding diametral pitch, divide 3.1416 by the circular pitch. Thus 1.57 P is the diametral pitch corresponding to 2-inch circular pitch, ($\frac{3.1416}{2}=P$).

Example. What diametral pitch corresponds to $\frac{1}{2}''$ circular pitch? Remembering that to divide by a fraction we multiply by the denominator and divide by the numerator, we obtain 6.28 as the quotient of 3.1416 divided by $\frac{1}{2}$. 6.28 P, then, is the diametral pitch corresponding to $\frac{1}{2}$ circular pitch. This means that in a gear of $\frac{1}{2}$ inch circular pitch there are six and twenty-eight one hundredths teeth to every inch in the diameter of the pitch circle. In the table of tooth parts the diametral pitches corresponding to circular pitches are carried out to four places of decimals, but in practice two places of decimals are enough.

When two gears are in mesh, so that their pitch circles just touch, the distance between their axes or centers is equal to the sum of the radii of the two gears. The number of *diameter* pitches between centers is equal to half the sum of number of teeth in both gears. This principle is the same as given in Chapter II., page 6, but when the diametral pitch and numbers of teeth in two gears are given, *add together the numbers of teeth in the two wheels and divide half the sum by the diametral pitch. The quotient is the center distance.* Rule to find Distance between Centers.

A gear of 20 teeth, 4 P, meshes with a gear of 50 teeth: what is the distance between their axes or centers? Adding 50 to 20 and dividing half the sum by 4, we obtain $8\frac{3}{4}''$ as the center distance. Example.

The term *diametral pitch* is also applied to a rack. Thus, a rack 3 P, means a rack that will mesh with a gear of 3 diametral pitch.

It will be seen that if the expression for a diameter pitch has any number except 1 for a numerator, we cannot express the diametral pitch by naming the denominator only. Thus, if the addendum or a diameter pitch is $\frac{4}{10}''$, the diametral pitch will be $2\frac{1}{2}$, because 1 divided by $\frac{4}{10}$ equals $2\frac{1}{2}$. Fractional Diametral Pitch.

CHAPTER VI.

SINGLE-CURVE GEARS HAVING LESS THAN 30 TEETH—GEARS AND RACKS TO MESH WITH GEARS HAVING LESS THAN 30 TEETH.

Construction, Fig. 10. In Fig. 10, the construction of the rack is the same as the construction of the rack in Chapter IV. The gear in Fig. 10 is drawn from base circle out to addendum circle, by the same method as the gear in Chapter III., but the spaces inside of base circle are drawn as follows:

Flanks of Gears in low numbers of Teeth. In gears, 12 and 13 teeth, the sides of spaces inside of base circle are parallel for a distance not more than $\frac{1}{8}$ of a diameter pitch, or $\frac{1}{8} s$; gears 14, 15 and 16 teeth not more than $\frac{1}{4} s$; 17 to 20 teeth, not more than $\frac{1}{2} s$. In gears with more than 20 teeth the parallel construction is omitted.

Construction of Fig. 10 continued. Then, with one leg of dividers in pitch circle in center of next tooth, e, and other leg just touching one of the parallel lines at b, continue the tooth side into c, until it will touch a fillet arc, whose radius is $\frac{1}{4}$ the width of space at the addendum circle. The part, $b'\ c'$, is an arc from center of tooth g, etc. The flanks of teeth or spaces in gear, Fig. 11, are made the same as those in Fig. 10.

This rule is merely conventional or not founded upon any principle other than the judgment of the designer, to effect the object to have spaces as wide as practicable, just below or inside of base circle, and then strengthen flank with as large a fillet as will clear addenda of any gear. If flanks in any gear will clear addenda of a rack, they will clear addenda of any

Internal Gear. other gear, except internal gears. An internal gear is one having teeth upon the inner side of a rim or ring. Now, it will be seen that the gear, Fig. 10, has teeth

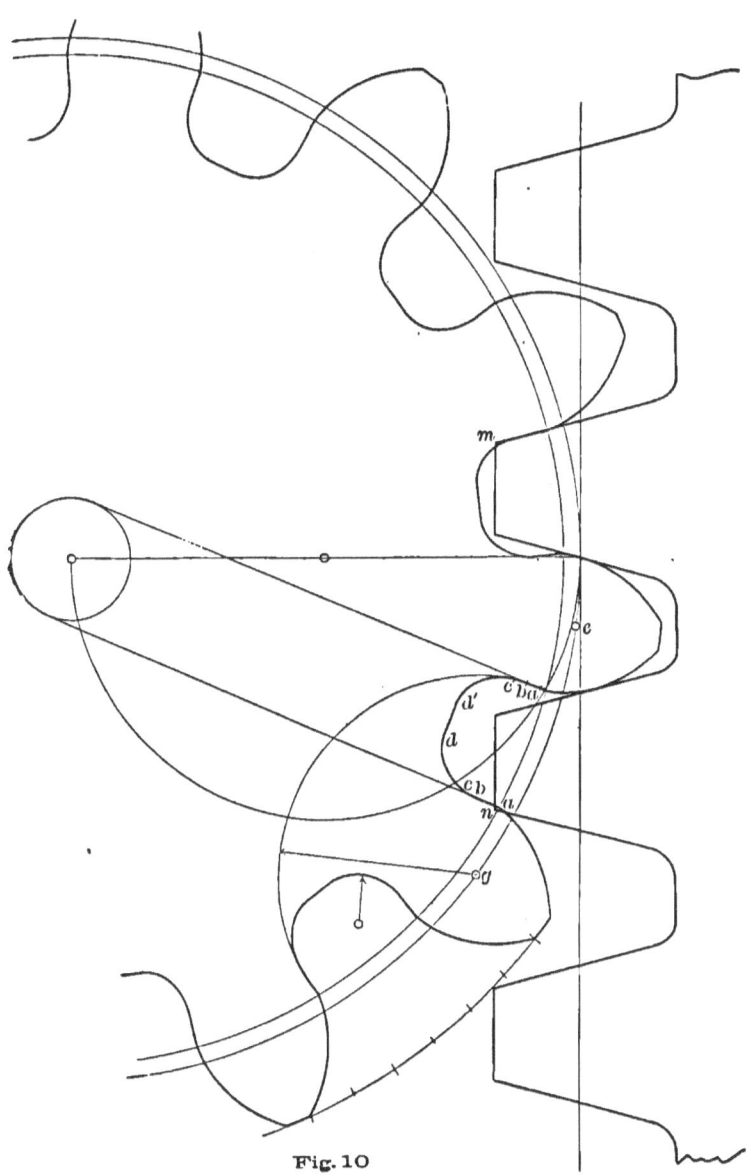

Fig. 10

too much rounded at the points or at the addendum circle. In gears of pitch coarser than 10 to inch (10 P), and having less than 30 teeth, this rounding becomes objectionable. This rounding occurs, because in these gears arcs of circles depart too far from the true involute curve, being so much that points of teeth get no bearing on flanks of teeth in other wheels.

Rounding of Addenda of Teeth.

In gear, Fig. 11, the teeth outside of base circle are made as nearly true involute as a workman will be able to get without special machinery. This is accomplished as follows: draw three or four tangents to the base circle, $i\ i'$, $j\ j'$, $k\ k'$, $l\ l'$, letting the points of tangency on base circle i', j', k', l' be about $\frac{1}{3}$ or $\frac{1}{4}$ the circular pitch apart; the first point, i', being distant from i, equal to $\frac{1}{4}$ the radius of pitch circle. With dividers set to $\frac{1}{4}$ the radius of pitch circle, placing one leg in i', draw the arc, $a'\ i\ j$; with one leg in j', and radius $j'\ j$, draw $j\ k$; with one leg in k', and radius $k'\ k$ draw $k\ l$. Should the addendum circle be outside of l, the tooth side can be completed with the last radius, $l'\ l$. The arcs, $a'\ i\ j$, $j\ k$ and $k\ l$, together form a very close approximation to a true involute from the base circle, $i'\ j'\ k'\ l'$. The *exact* involute for gear teeth is the curve made by the end of a band when unwound from a cylinder of the same diameter as base circle.

Approxima- tion to True Involute.

The foregoing operation of drawing tooth sides, although tedious in description, is very easy of practical application.

Rounding of Addenda of Rack.

It will also be seen that the addenda of rack teeth in Fig. 10, interfere with the gear-teeth flanks, as at $m\ n$; to avoid this interference, the teeth of rack, Fig. 11, are rounded at points or addenda.

It is also necessary to round off the points of involute teeth in high-numbered gears, when they are to interchange with low-numbered gears. In interchangeable sets of gears the lowest-numbered pinion is usually 12. Just how much to round off is best learnt by making templets of a few teeth out of thin metal or cardboard, for the gear and rack, or, two gears required, and fitting addenda of teeth to clear flanks. However accurate we may make a diagram, it is quite

Templets necessary for Rounding off Points of teeth.

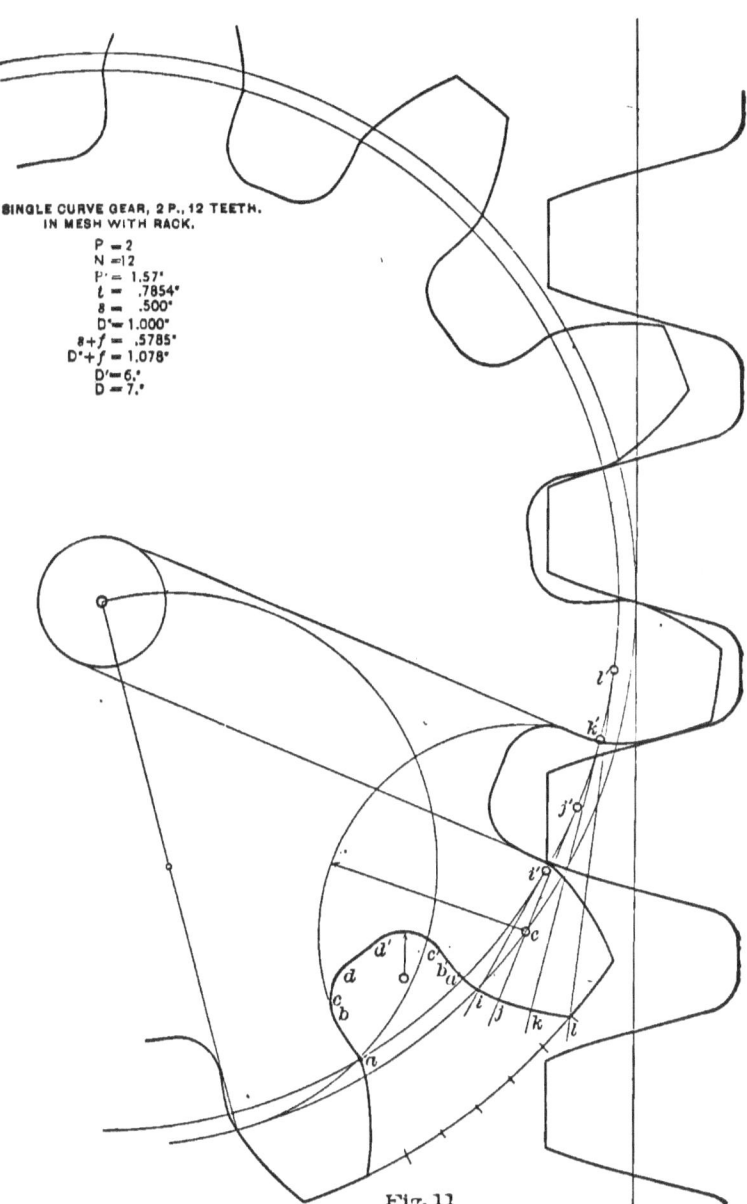

SINGLE CURVE GEAR, 2 P., 12 TEETH.
IN MESH WITH RACK.
P = 2
N = 12
P' = 1.57"
t = .7854"
s = .500"
D' = 1.000"
s+f = .5785"
D'+f = 1.078"
D'= 6."
D = 7."

Fig. 11

as well to make templets in order to shape cutters accurately.

Diagrams for a Set of Cutters. It is best to make cutters to corrected diagrams, as in Fig. 11. When corrected diagrams are made, as in Fig. 11, take the following:

For 12 and 13 teeth, diagram of 12 teeth.
" 14 to 16 " " " 14 "
" 17 " 20 " " " 17 "
" 21 " 25 " " " 21 "
" 26 " 34 " " " 26 "
" 35 " 54 " " " 35 "
" 55 " 134 " " " 55 "
" 135 " rack, " " "135 "

Templets for large gears must be fitted to run with 12 teeth, etc.

CHAPTER VII.

DOUBLE-CURVE TEETH—GEAR, 15 TEETH—RACK.

In double-curve teeth the formation of tooth sides changes at the pitch line. In all gears the part of teeth outside of pitch line is convex; in some gears the sides of teeth inside pitch line are convex; in some, radial; in others, concave. Convex faces and concave flanks are most familiar to mechanics. In interchangeable sets of gears, *one* gear in each set, or of each pitch, has radial flanks. In the best practice, *this gear has fifteen teeth.* Gears with more than fifteen teeth, have concave flanks; gears with less than fifteen teeth, have convex flanks. Fifteen teeth is called the *Base* of this system.   *All Double-curve Tooth Faces are Convex.*

We will first draw a gear of fifteen teeth. This fifteen-tooth construction enters into gears of any number of teeth and also into racks. Let the gear be 3 P. Having obtained data, we proceed as follows: *Construction of Fig. 12.*

1. Draw pitch circle and point it off into parts equal to one-thirtieth of the circumference, or equal to thickness of tooth = t.

2. From the center, through one of these points, as at T, Fig. 12, draw line O T A. Draw addendum and whole-depth circles.

3. About this point, T, with same radius as 15-tooth pitch circle, describe arcs A K and O k. For any other double-curve gear of 3 P., the radius of arcs, A K and O k, will be the same as in this 15-tooth gear = $2\frac{1}{2}''$. In a 15-tooth gear, the arc, O k, passes through the center O, but for a gear having any other number of teeth, this construction arc does not pass through center of gear. Of course, the 15-tooth radius of arcs, A K and O k, is always taken from the pitch we are working with.

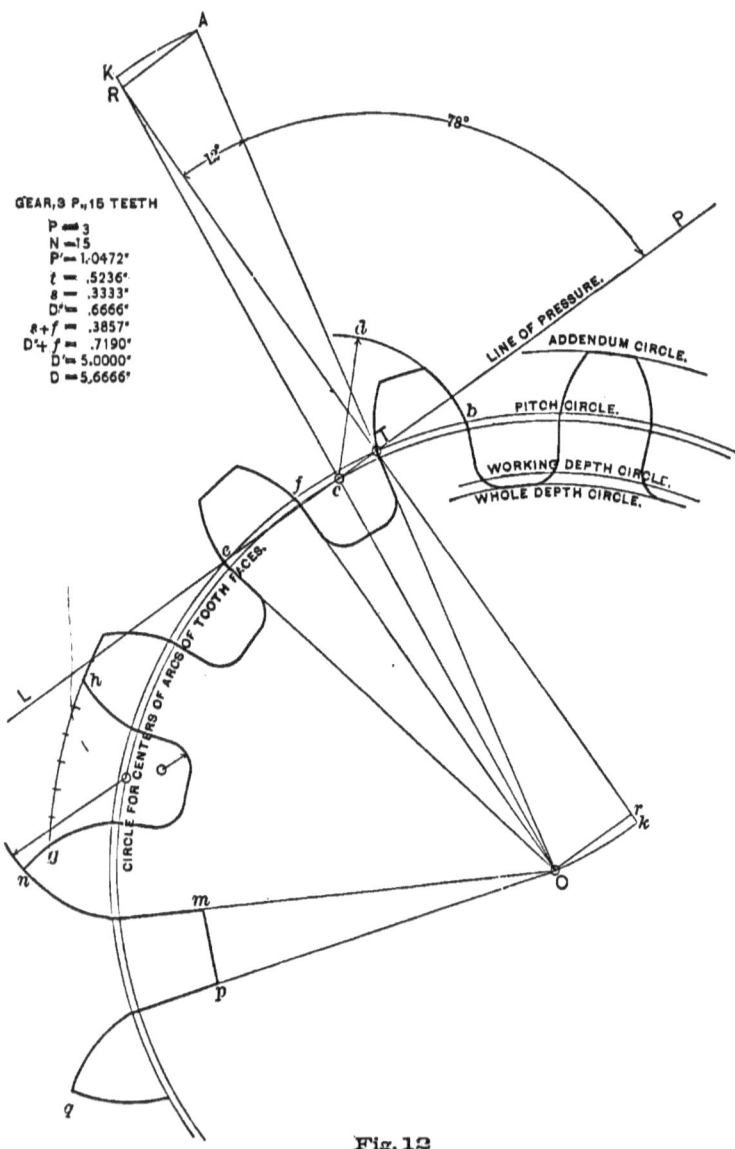

Fig. 12
DOUBLE CURVE GEAR.

4. Upon these arcs on opposite sides of lines O T A, lay off tooth thickness, A K and O k, and draw line K T k.

5. Perpendicular to K T k, draw line of pressure, L T P; also through O and A, draw lines A R and O r, perpendicular to K T k. The line of pressure is at an angle of 78° with the radius of gear.

6. From O, draw a line O R to intersection of A R with K T k. Through point c, where O R intersects L P, describe a circle about the center, O. *In this circle one leg of dividers is placed to describe tooth faces*

7. The radius, c d, of arc of tooth faces is the straight distance from c to tooth-thickness point, b, on the other side of radius, O T. With this radius, c b, describe both sides of tooth faces.

8. Draw flanks of all teeth radial, as O e and O f. The *base gear*, 15 *teeth* only, has radial flanks.

9. With radius equal to one sixth of the widest part of space, as g h, draw fillets at bottom of teeth.

The foregoing is a close approximation to epicycloidal teeth. To get exact teeth, make two 15-tooth gears of thin metal. Make addenda long enough to come to a point, as at n and q. Make radial flanks, as at m and p, deep enough to clear addenda when gears are in mesh. First finish the flanks, then fit the long addenda to the flanks when gears are in mesh. *Approximation to Epicycloidal Teeth.*

When these two templet gears are alike, the centers are the right distance apart and the teeth interlock without backlash, they are exact. One of these templet gears can now be used to test any other templet gear of the same pitch. *Standard Templets.*

Gears and racks will be right when they run correctly with one of these 15-tooth templet gears. Five or six teeth are enough to make in a gear templet.

DOUBLE-CURVE RACK.—Let us draw a rack 3 P. *Double-curve Rack, Fig. 13.* Having obtained data of teeth we proceed as follows:

1. Draw pitch line and point it off in parts equal to one-half the circular pitch. Draw addendum and whole-depth lines.

2. Through one of the points, as at T, Fig. 13, draw line O T A perpendicular to pitch line of rack.

28 BROWN & SHARPE MFG. CO.

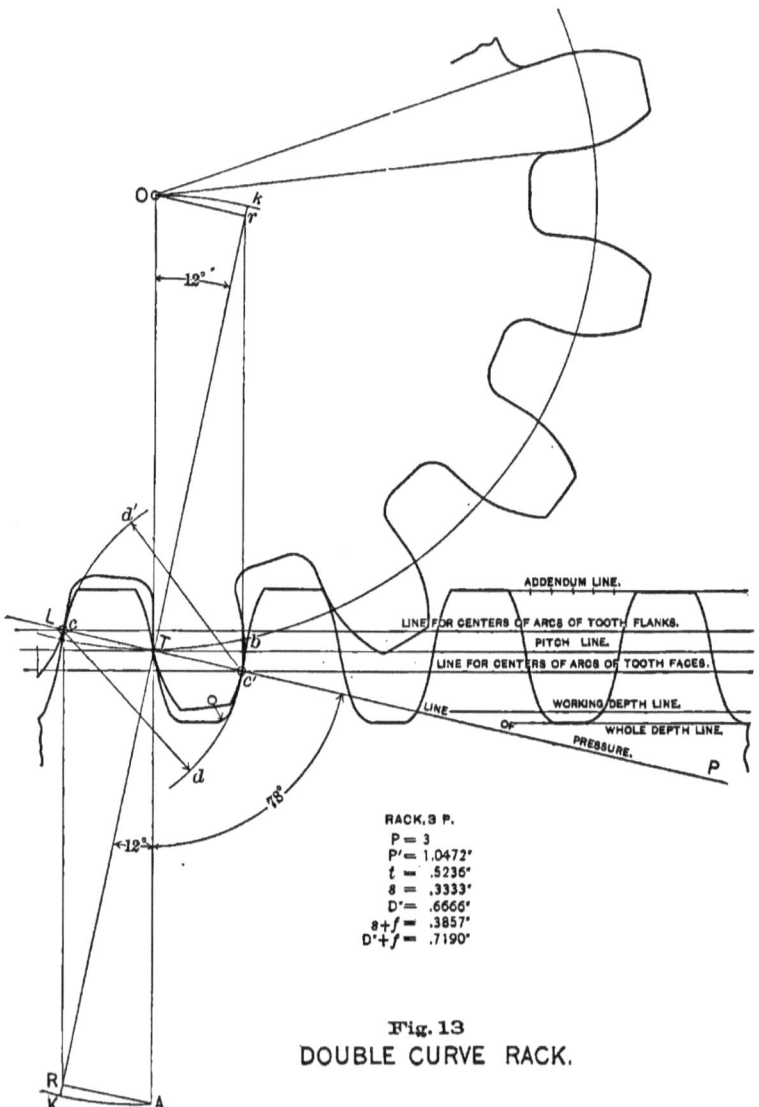

RACK, 3 P.
P = 3
P' = 1.0472"
t = .5236"
s = .3333"
D' = .6666"
s+f = .3857"
D'+f = .7190"

Fig. 13
DOUBLE CURVE RACK.

3. About T make precisely the same construction as was made about T in Fig. 12. That is, with radius of 15-tooth pitch circle and center T draw arcs O k and A K; make O k and A K equal to tooth thickness; draw K T k; draw O r, A R, and line of pressure, each perpendicular to K T k.

4. Through R and r, draw lines parallel to O A. Through intersections c and c' of these lines, with pressure line L P, draw lines parallel to pitch line.

5. In these last lines place leg of dividers, and draw faces and flanks of teeth as in sketch.

6. The radius c' d' of rack-tooth faces is the same length as radius c d of rack-tooth flanks, and is the straight distance from c to tooth-thickness point b on opposite side of line O A.

7. The radius for fillet at bottom of rack teeth is equal to ¼ of the widest part of tooth space. This radius can be varied to suit the judgment of the designer, so long as a fillet does not interfere with teeth of engaging gear.

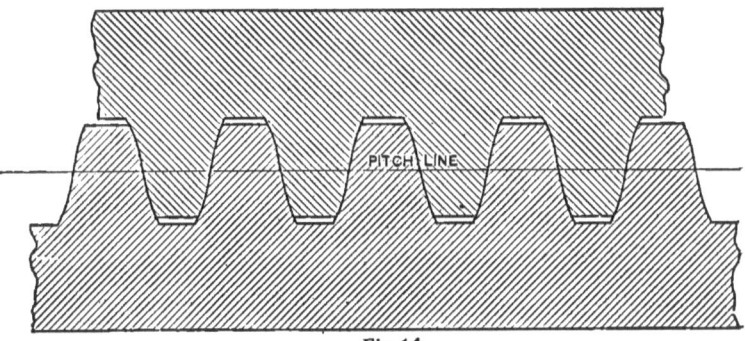

Fig. 14

Racks of the same pitch, to mesh with interchangeable gears, should be alike when placed side by side, and fit each other when placed together as in Fig. 14.

In Fig. 13, a few teeth of a 15-tooth wheel are shown in mesh with the rack.

CHAPTER VIII.

DOUBLE-CURVE GEARS, HAVING MORE AND LESS THAN 15 TEETH—ANNULAR GEARS.

Construction of Fig. 15. Let us draw two gears, 12 and 24 teeth, 4 P, in mesh. In Fig. 15 the construction lines of the lower or 24-tooth gear are full. The upper or 12-tooth gear construction lines are dotted. The line of pressure, L P, and the line K T k answer for both gears. The arcs A K and O k are described about T. The radius of these arcs is the radius of pitch circle of a gear 15 teeth 4 pitch. The length of arcs A K and O k is the tooth thickness for 4 P. The line K T k is obtained the same as in Chapter VII. for all double-curve gears, the distances only varying as the pitch. Having drawn the pitch circles, the line K T k, and, perpendicular to K T k, the lines A R, O r and the line of pressure L T P, we proceed with the 24-tooth gear as follows:

1. From center C, through r, draw line intersecting line of pressure in m. Also draw line from center C to R, crossing the line of pressure L P at c.

2. Through m describe circle concentric with pitch circle about C. This is the circle in which to place one leg of dividers to describe flanks of teeth.

3. The radius, $m\ n$, of flanks is the straight distance from m to the first tooth-thickness point on other side of line of centers, C C', at v. The arc is continued to n, to show how constructed. This method of obtaining radius of double-curve tooth flanks applies to all gears having more than fifteen teeth.

4. The construction of tooth faces is similar to 15-tooth wheel in Chapter VII. That is: Draw a circle through c concentric to pitch circle; in this circle place one leg of dividers to draw tooth faces, the radius of tooth faces being $c\ b$.

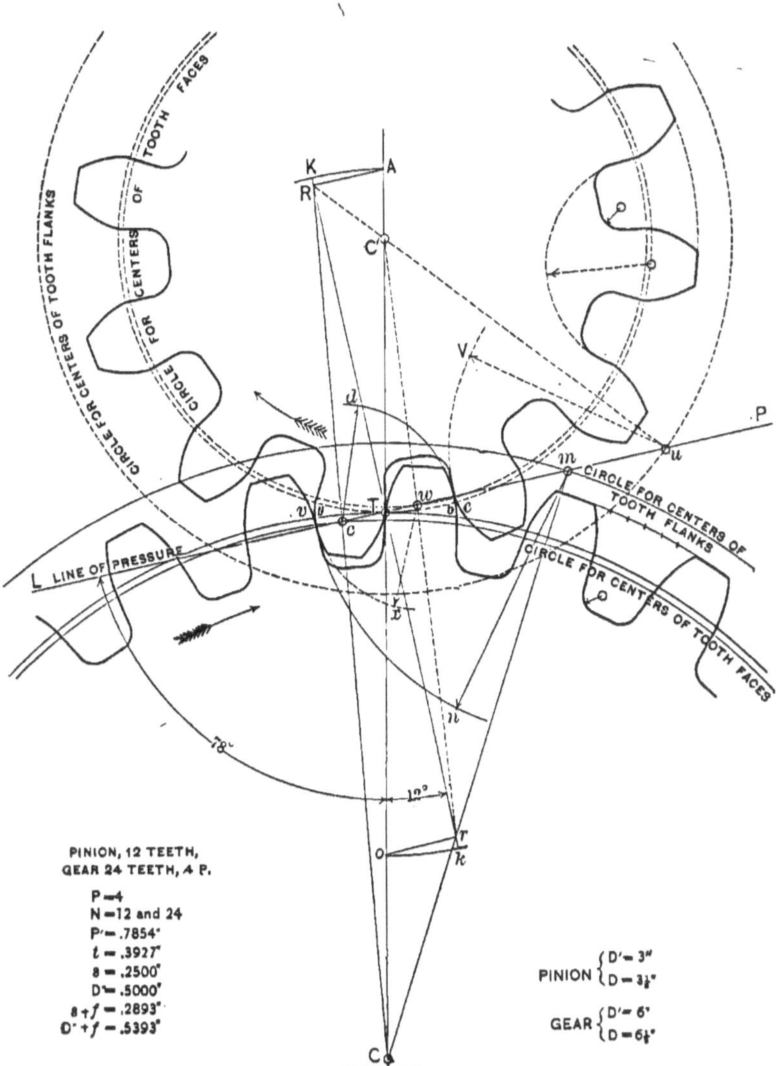

PROVIDENCE, R. I.   31

PINION, 12 TEETH,
GEAR 24 TEETH, 4 P.

P = 4
N = 12 and 24
P' = .7854"
t = .3927"
s = .2500"
D" = .5000"
s + f = .2893"
D" + f = .5393"

PINION $\begin{cases} D' = 3" \\ D = 3\frac{1}{4}" \end{cases}$

GEAR $\begin{cases} D' = 6" \\ D = 6\frac{1}{4}" \end{cases}$

Fig. 15.
DOUBLE CURVE GEARS IN MESH.

5. The radius of fillets at roots of teeth is equal to one-sixth the width of space at addendum circle.

The constructions for flanks of 12, 13 and 14 teeth are similar to each other and as follows:

1. Through center, C', draw line from R, intersecting line of pressure in u. Through u draw circle about C'. In this circle one leg of dividers is placed for drawing flanks.

2. The radius of flanks is the distance from u to the first tooth-thickness point, e, on the *same side* of C T C'. This gives convex flanks. The arc is continued to V, to show construction.

3. This arc for flanks is continued in or toward the center, only about one-sixth of the working depth (or $\frac{1}{3}$ s.); the lower part of flank is similar to flanks of gear in Chapter VI.

4. The faces are similar to those in 15-tooth gear, Chapter VII., and to the 24-tooth gear in the foregoing, the radius being $w\ y$; the arc is continued to x, to show construction.

ANNULAR GEARS. Gears with teeth inside of a rim or ring are called Annular or Internal Gears. The construction of tooth outlines is similar to the foregoing, but the *spaces* of a spur external gear become the *teeth* of an annular gear.

Prof. MacCord has shown that in the system just described, the pinion meshing with an annular gear, must differ from it by *at least* fifteen teeth. Thus, a gear of 24 teeth cannot work with an annular gear of 36 teeth, but it will work with annular gears of 39 teeth and more. An annular gear differing from its mate by less than 15 teeth can be made. This will be shown in Part II.

Annular-gear patterns require more clearance for moulding than external or spur gears.

In speaking of different-sized gears, the smallest ones are often called "pinions."

The angle of pressure in all gears except involute, constantly changes. 78° is the pressure angle in double-curve, or epicycloidal gears for an instant only; in our example, it is 78° when one side of a tooth reaches the line of centers, and the pressure against teeth is applied in the direction of the arrows.

The pressure angle of involute gears does not change. An explanation of the term angle of pressure is given in Part II.

We obtain the forms for epicycloidal gear cutters by means of a machine called the Odontom Engine. This machine will cut original gears with theoretical accuracy.

It has been thought best to make 24 gear cutters for each pitch. This enables us to fill any requirement of gear-cutting very closely, as the range covered by any one cutter is so small that it is exceedingly near to the exact shape of all gears so covered.

24 Double curve Gear Cutters for each Pitch.

Of course, a cutter can be *exactly* right for only one gear. Special cutters can be made, if desired.

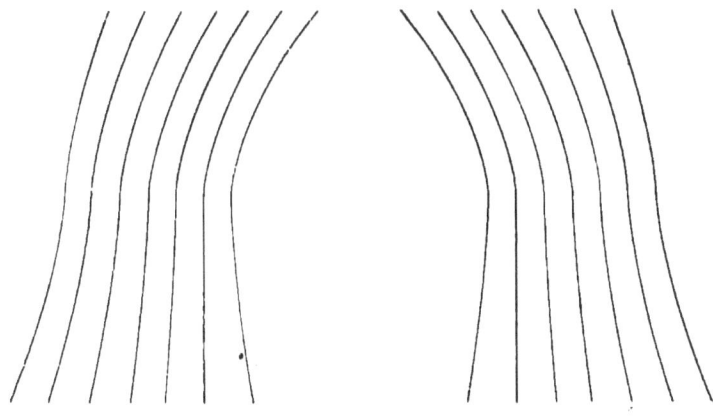

1 PITCH TOOTH CURVES
from the
ODONTOM ENGINE.

CHAPTER IX.
BEVEL-GEAR BLANKS.

Teeth of Bevel Gears formed upon frustrums of cones.

Bevel Gears connect shafts whose axes meet when sufficiently prolonged. The teeth of bevel gears are formed about the frustrums of cones whose apexes are at the same point where the shafts meet. In Fig. 16 we have the axes A O and B O, meeting at O, and the apexes of the cones also at O. These cones are called the pitch cones, because they roll upon each other, and because upon them the teeth are pitched. If, in any bevel gear, the teeth were sufficiently prolonged toward the apex, they would become infinitely small; that is, the teeth would all end in a point, or vanish at O. We can also consider a bevel gear as beginning at the apex and becoming larger and larger as we go away from the apex. Hence, as the bevel gear teeth are tapering from end to end, we may say

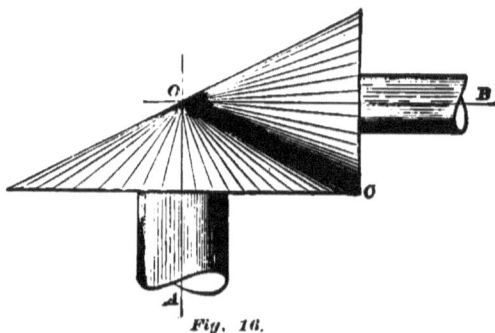

Fig. 16.

that a bevel gear has a number of pitches and pitch circles, or diameters; in speaking of the pitch of a bevel gear, we mean always the pitch at the largest pitch circle, or at the largest pitch diameter, as at b d, Fig. 17.

Fig. 17 is a section of three bevel gears, the gear o B q being twice as large as the two others. The outer surface of a tooth as m m' is called the face of the tooth. The distance m m' is usually called the length of the face of the tooth, though the real length is the distance that it occupies upon the line O i. The outer part of a tooth at m n is called its large end, and the inner part m' n' the small end.

<small>Construction of Bevel Gear Blanks.</small>

Almost all bevel gears connect shafts that are at right angles with each other, and unless stated otherwise we always understand that they are so wanted.

The directions given in connection with Fig. 17 apply to gears with axes at right angles.

Having decided upon the pitch and the numbers of teeth:—

1. Draw centre lines of shafts, A O B and C O D, at right angles.

2. Parallel to A O B, draw lines a b and c d, each distant from A O B, equal to half the largest pitch diameter of one gear. For 24 teeth, 4 pitch, this half largest pitch diameter is 3".

3. Parallel to C O D, draw lines e f and g h, distant from C O D, equal to half the largest pitch diameter of the other gear. For a gear, 12 teeth, 4 pitch, this half largest pitch diameter is $1\frac{1}{2}$".

4. At the intersection of these four lines, draw lines O i, O j, O k, and O l; these lines give the size and shape of pitch cones. We call them "Cone Pitch Lines."

5. Perpendicular to the cone-pitch lines and through the intersection of lines a b, c d, e f, and g h, draw lines m n, o p, q r. We have drawn also u v to show that another gear can be drawn from the same diagram. Four gears, two of each size, can be drawn from this diagram.

6. Upon the lines m n, o p, q r, the addenda and depth of the teeth are laid off, these lines passing

through the largest pitch circle of the gears. Lay off the addendum, it being in these gears ¼". This gives distance m n, o p, q r, and u v equal to the working depth of teeth, which in these gears is ½". The addendum of course is measured perpendicularly from the cone pitch lines as at k r.

7. Draw lines O m, O n, O p, O o, O q, O r. These lines give the height of teeth above the cone-pitch lines as they approach O, and would vanish entirely at O. It is quite as well never to have the length of teeth, or face, m n' longer than one-third the apex distance m O, nor more than two and one-half times the circular pitch.

8. Having decided upon the length of face, draw limiting lines m'n' perpendicular to i O, q' r' perpendicular to k O, and so on.

The distance between the cone-pitch lines at the inner ends of the teeth m' n' and q' r' is called the inner or smaller pitch diameter, and the circle at these points is called the smallest pitch circle. We now have the outline of a section of the gears through their axes. The distance m r is the whole diameter of the pinion.

The Whole Diameter of Bevel-Gear Blanks can be obtained by Measuring Drawings.

The distance q o is the whole diameter of the gear. In practice these diameters can be obtained by measuring the drawing. The diameter of pinion is 3.45" and of the gear 6.22". We can find the angles also by measuring the drawing with a protractor. In the absence of a protractor, templetes can be cut to the drawing. The angle formed by line m m' with a b is the angle of face of pinion, in this pinion 59° 11', or 59¼° nearly. The lines q q' and g h give us angle of face of gear, for this gear 22° 19', or 22⅓° nearly The angle formed by m n with a b is called the angle of edge of pinion, in our sketch 26° 31', or about 26¼°. The angle of edge of gear, line q r with g h, is 63° 26', or about 63¼°. In turning blanks to these angles we place one arm of the protractor or templet against the end of the hub, when trying angles of a blank. Some designers give the angles from the axes of gears, but

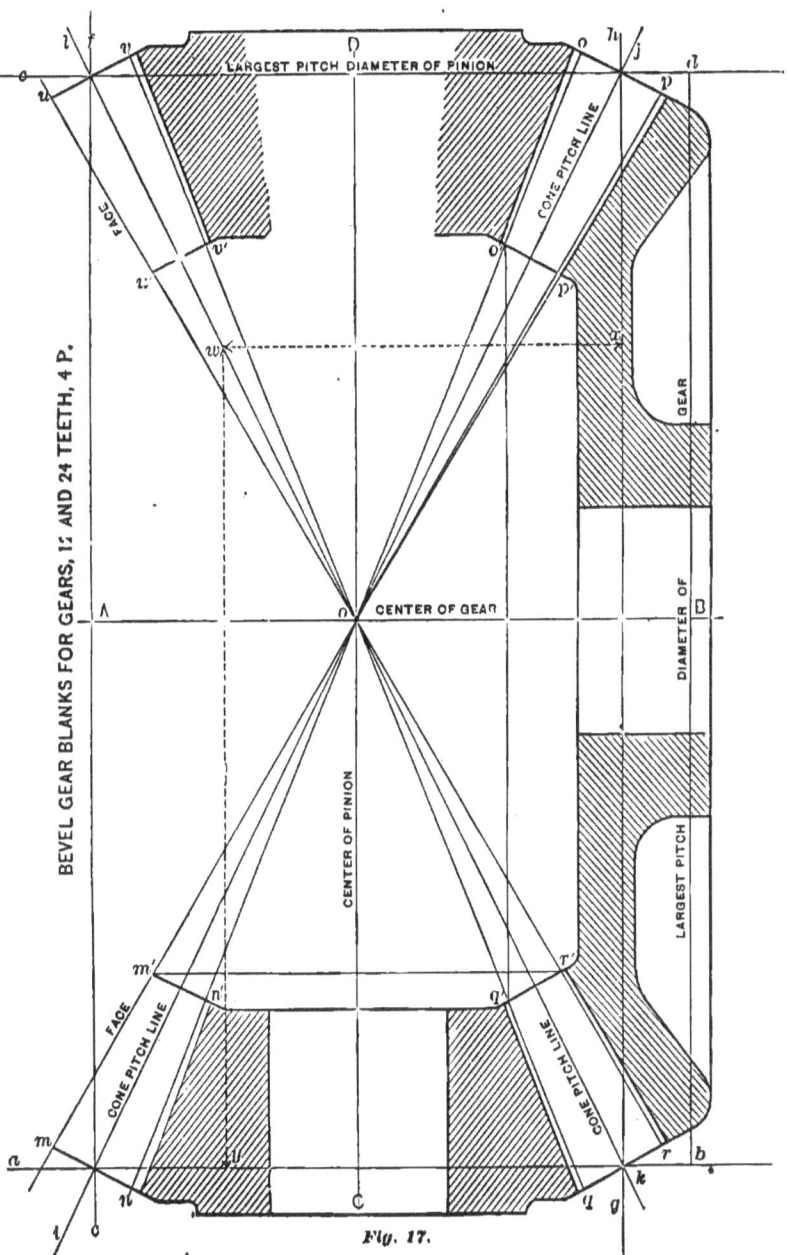

Fig. 17.

it is not convenient to try blanks in this way. The method that we have given comes right also for angles as figures in compound rests.

When axes are at right angles, the sum of angles of edge in the two gears equals 90°, and the sums of angle of edge and face in each gear are alike.

The angles of the axes remaining the same, all pairs of bevel gears of the same ratio have the same angle of edge; all pairs of same ratio and of same numbers of teeth have the same angles of both edges and faces independent of the pitch. Thus, in all pairs of bevel gears having one gear twice as large as the other, with axes at right angles, the angle of edge of large gear is 63° 26', and the angle of edge of small gear is 26° 34'.

In all pairs of bevel gears with axes at right angles, one gear having 24 teeth and the other gear having 12 teeth, the angle of face of small gear is 59° 11'.

Another method of obtaining Whole Diameter of Blanks. The following method of obtaining the whole diameter of bevel gears is sometimes preferred:

From k lay off; upon the cone-pitch line, a distance K w, equal to ten times the working depth of the teeth $= 10\ D''$. Now add $\frac{1}{6}$ of the shortest distance of w from the line g h, which is the perpendicular dotted line w x, to the outside pitch diameter of gear, and the sum will be the whole diameter of gear. In the same manner $\frac{1}{6}$ of w y, added to the outside pitch diameter of pinion, gives the whole diameter of pinion. The part added to the pitch diameter is called the *diameter increment*.

Part II gives trigonometrical methods of figuring bevel gears: in our Formulas in Gearing there are trigonometrical formulas for bevel gears, and also tables for angles and sizes.

Construction of Bevel-Gear Blanks whose Axes are not at Right Angles. A somewhat similar construction will do for bevel gears whose axes are not at right angles.

In Fig. 18 the axes are shown at O B and O D, the angle B O D being less than a right angle.

1. Parallel to O B, and at a distance from it equal to the radius of the gear, we draw the lines a b and c d.

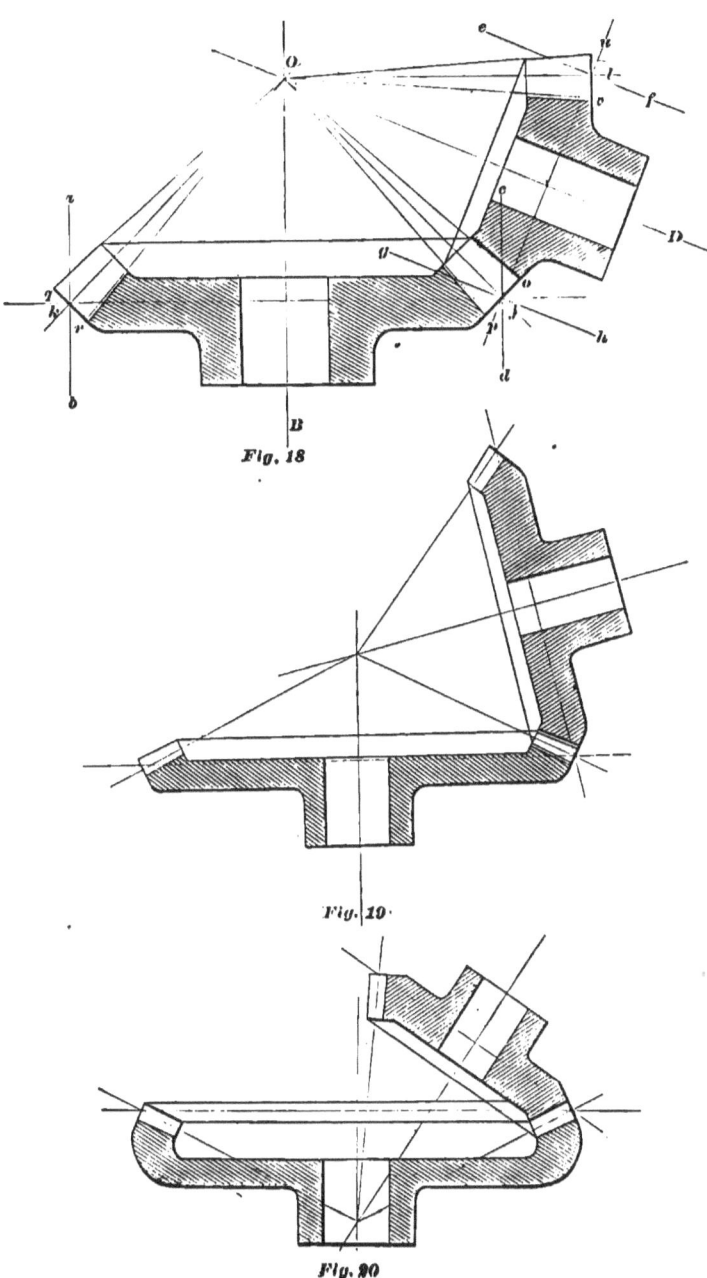

Fig. 18

Fig. 19

Fig. 20

2. Parallel to O D, and at a distance from it equal to the radius of the pinion, we draw the lines e f and g h.

3. Now, through the point j at the intersection of c d and g h, we draw a line perpendicular to O B. This line k j, limited by a b and c d, represents the largest pitch diameter of the gear.

Through j we draw a line perpendicular to O D. This line j l, limited by e f and g h, represents the largest pitch diameter of the pinion.

4. Through the point k at the intersection of a b with k j, we draw a line to O, a line from j to O, and another from l, at the intersection j l and e f to O. These lines O k, O j, and O l, represent the cone-pitch lines, as in Fig. 17.

5. Perpendicular to the cone-pitch lines we draw the lines u v, o p, and q r. Upon these lines we lay off the addenda and working depth as in the previous figure, and then draw lines to the point O as before.

By a similar construction Figs. 19 and 20 can be drawn.

STOCKING CUTTER.

CHAPTER X.
BEVEL GEARS.
FORMS AND SIZES OF TEETH.
CUTTING TEETH.

To obtain the form of the teeth in a bevel gear we do not lay them out upon a pitch circle, as we do in a spur gear, because the rolling pitch surface of a bevel gear, at any point, is of a longer radius of curvature than the actual radius of a pitch circle that passes through that point. Thus in Fig. 21, let f g c be a cone about the axis O A, the diameter of the cone being f c, and its radius g c. Now the radius of curvature of the surface, at c, is evidently longer than g c, as can be seen in the other view at C ; the full line shows the curvature of the surface, and the dotted line shows the curvature of a circle of the radius g c. It is extremely difficult to represent the exact form of bevel gear teeth upon a flat surface, because a bevel gear is essentially spherical in its nature ; for practical purposes we draw a line c A perpendicular to O c, letting c A reach the centre line O A, and take c A as the radius of a circle upon which to lay out the teeth. This is shown at c n m, Fig. 22. For convenience the line c A is sometimes called the back cone radius. Form of bevel gear teeth.

Let us take, for an example, a bevel gear and a pinion 24 and 18 teeth, 5 pitch, shafts at right angles. To obtain the forms of the teeth and the data for cutting, we need to draw a section of only a half of each gear, as in Fig. 22. Example, Fig. 22.

1. Draw the centre lines A O and B O, then the lines g h and c d, and the gear blank lines as described in Chapter IX. Extend the lines o' p' and o p until they meet the centre lines at A' B' and A B.

2. With the radius A c draw the arc c n m, which we take as the geometrical pitch circle upon which to lay out the teeth at the large end. The distance A' c' is taken as the radius of the geometrical pitch circle at the small end; to avoid confusion an arc of this circle is drawn at c" n' m' about A.

3. For the pinion we have the radius B c for the geometrical pitch circle at the large end and B' c' for the small end: the distance B' c' is transferred to B c'''.

4. Upon the arc c n m lay off spaces equal to the tooth thickness at the large pitch circle, which in our example is .314". Draw the outlines of the teeth as in previous chapters: for single curve teeth we draw a semi-circle upon the radius A c, and proceed as described in chapter III. For all bevel gears that are to be cut with a rotary disk cutter, or a common gear cutter, single curve teeth are chosen; and no attempt should be made to cut double curve teeth. Double curve teeth can be drawn by the directions given in chapters VII and VIII. We now have the form of the teeth at the large end of the gear. Repeat this operation with the radius B C about B, and we have the form of the teeth at the large end of the pinion.

5. The tooth parts at the small end are designated by the same letters as at the large, with the addition of an accent mark to each letter, as in the right hand column, Fig. 22, the clearance, f, however, is usually the same at the small end as at the large, for convenience in cutting the teeth.

Sizes of the tooth parts. The sizes of the tooth parts at the small end are in the same proportion to those at the large end as the line O c' is to O c. In our example O c' is 2", and O c is 3"; dividing O c' by O c we have $\frac{2}{3}$, or .666, as the ratio of the sizes at the small end to those

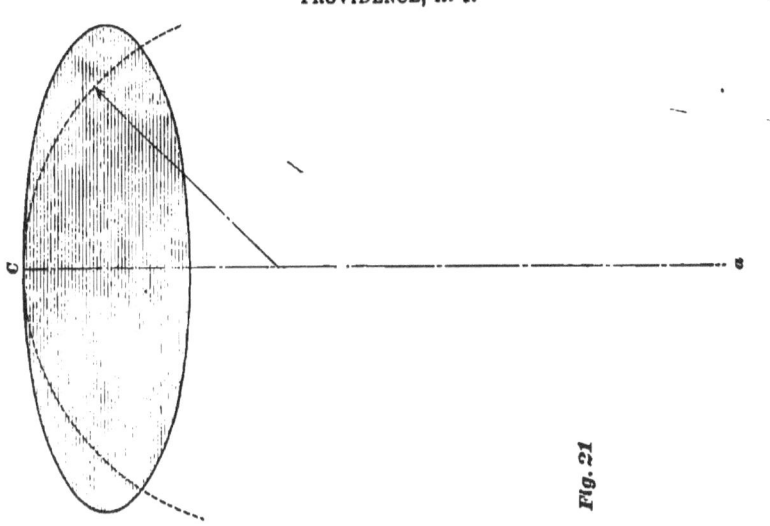

Fig. 21

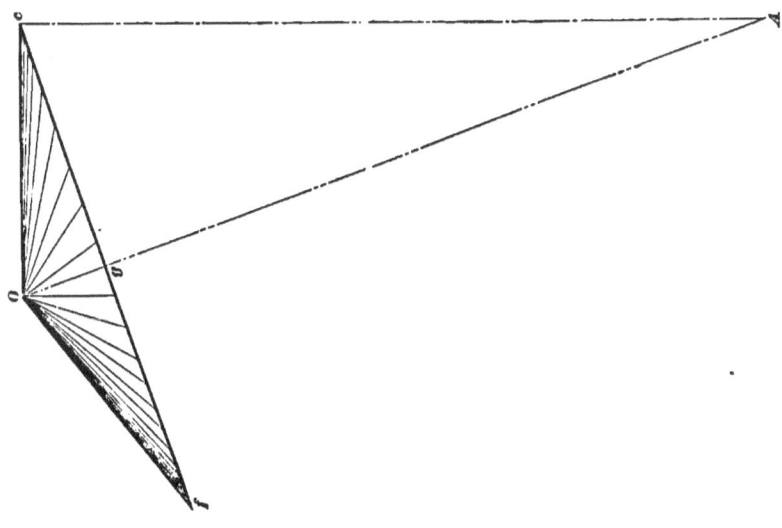

at the large: t' is .209" or ⅔ of .314", and so on. If the distance n m is equal to the outer tooth thickness, t, upon the arc c n m, the lines n A and m A will be a distance apart equal to the inner tooth thickness t' upon the arc $c''\, n'\, m'$. The addendum, s', and the working depth, D''', are at $o'\, c'$ and $o'\, p'$.

6. Upon the arcs $c''\, n'\, m'$ and c''' we draw the forms of the teeth of the gear and pinion at the inside.

Example of Cutting. As an example of the cutting of bevel gears with rotary disk cutters, or common gear cutters, let us take a pair of 8 pitch, 12 and 24 teeth, shown in Fig. 23.

Length of tooth face. In making the drawing it is well to remember that nothing is gained by having the face F E longer than five times the thickness of the teeth at the large pitch circle, and that even this is too long when it is more than a third of the *apex distance* O c. To cut a bevel gear with a rotary cutter, as in Fig. 24, is at best but a compromise, because the teeth change pitch from end to end, so that the cutter, being of the right form for the large ends of the teeth can not be right for the small ends, and the variation is too great when the length of face is greater than a third of the apex distance O c, Fig. 23. In the example, one-third of the apex distance is $\tfrac{9}{16}''$, but F E is drawn only a half inch, which even though rather short, has changed the pitch from 8 at the outside to finer than 11 at the inside. Frequently the teeth have to be rounded over at the small ends by filing; the longer the teeth the more we have to file. If there is any doubt about the strength of the teeth, it is better to lengthen at the large end, and make the pitch coarser rather than to lengthen at the small end.

Data for cutting. These data are needed before beginning to cut:

1. The pitch and the numbers of the teeth the same as for spur gears.

2. The data for the cutter, as to its form: sometimes two cutters are needed for a pair of bevel gears.

3. The whole depth of the tooth spaces, both at

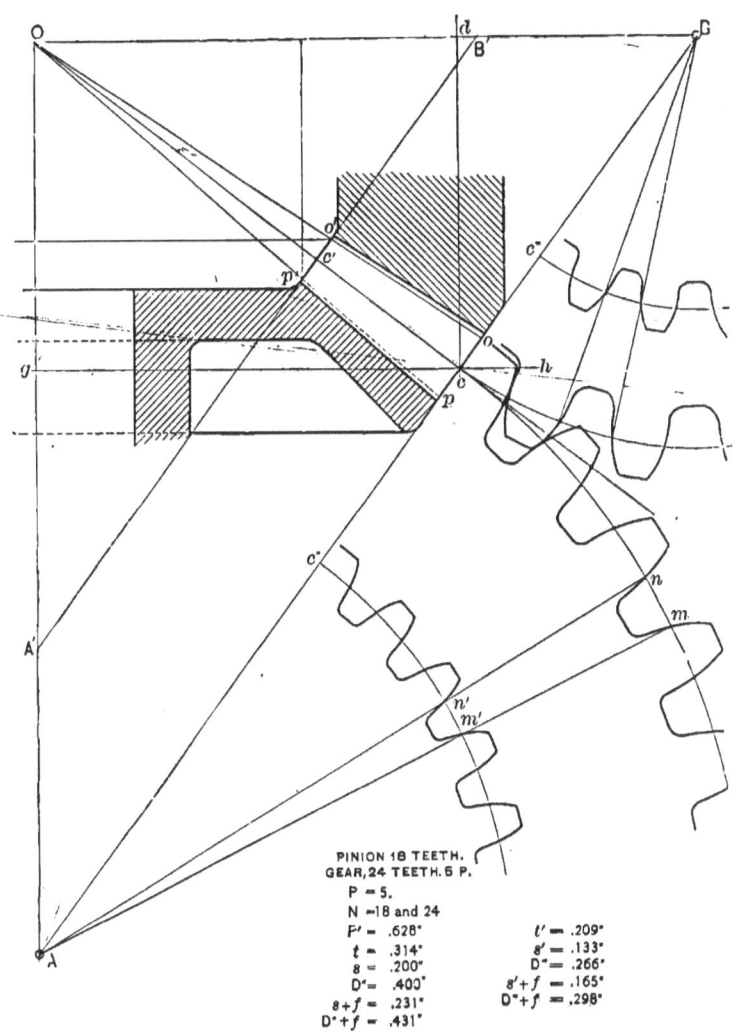

PINION 18 TEETH.
GEAR, 24 TEETH. 5 P.
P = 5.
N = 18 and 24
P' = .628"
t = .314"
s = .200"
D' = .400"
s+f = .231"
D'+f = .431"
t' = .209"
s' = .133"
D" = .266"
s'+f = .165"
D"+f = .298"

Fig. 29.

BEVEL GEARS, FORM AND SIZE OF TEETH.

the outside and inside ends; $D'' + f$ at the outside, and $D''' + f$ at the inside.

4. The thickness of the teeth at the outside and at the inside; t and t'.

5. The height of the teeth above the pitch lines at the outside and inside; s and s'.

6. The cutting angles, or the angles that the path of the cutter makes with the axes of the gears. In Fig. 23 the cutting angle for the gear c D is A Op, and the cutting angle for the pinion is B O o.

Selection of cutters. The form of the teeth in one of these gears differs so much from that in the other gear that two cutters are required. In determining these cutters we do not have to develop the forms of the gear teeth as in Fig. 22; we need merely measure the lines A c and B c, Fig. 23, and calculate the cutter forms as if these distances were the radii of the pitch circles of the gears to be cut. Twice the length A c, in inches, multiplied by the diametral pitch, equals the number of teeth for which to select a cutter tor the twenty-four-tooth gear: this number is about 54, which calls for a number three bevel gear cutter in the list of bevel gear cutters, page 61. Twice B c, multiplied by 8, equals about 13, which indicates a No. 8 bevel gear cutter for the pinion. This method of selecting cutters is based upon the idea of shaping the teeth as nearly right as practicable at the large end, and then filing the small ends where the cutter has not rounded them over enough.

In Fig. 25 the tooth L has been cut to thickness at both the outer and inner pitch lines, but it must still be rounded at the inner end. The teeth M M have been filed. In thus rounding the teeth they should not be filed thinner at the pitch lines.

There are several things that affect the shape of the teeth, so that the choice of cutters is not always so simple a matter as the taking of the lines A c and B c as radii.

In cutting a bevel gear, in the ordinary gear cutting

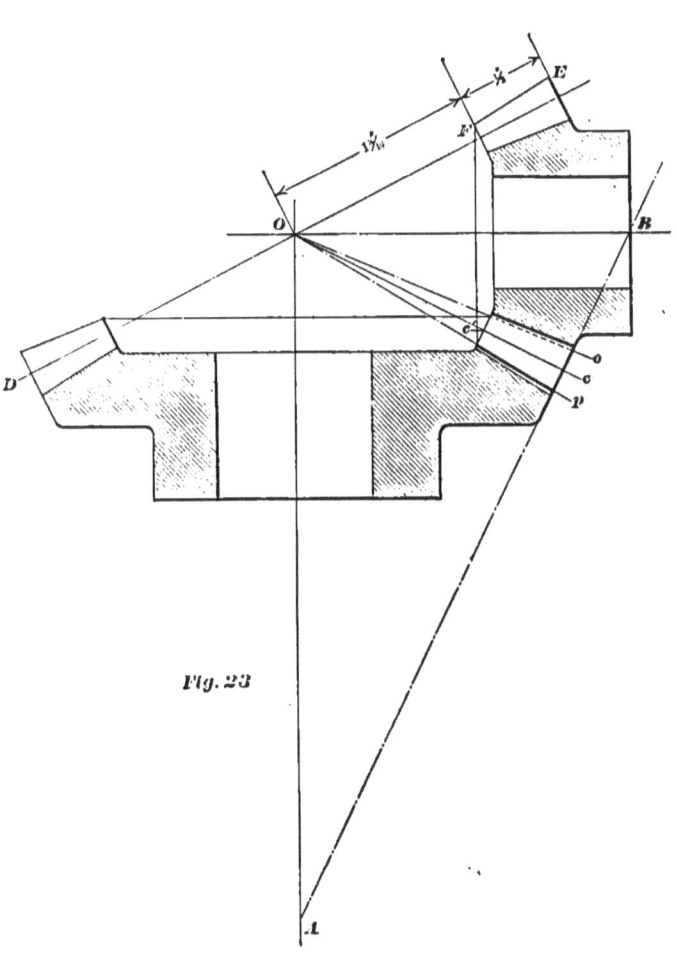

Fig. 23

machines, the finished spaces are not always of the same form as the cutter might be expected to make, because of the changes in the positions of the cutter and of the gear blank in order to cut the teeth of the right thickness at both ends. The cutter must of course be thin enough to pass through the small end of the spaces, so that the large end has to be cut to the right width by adjusting either the cutter or the blank sidewise, then rotating the blank and cutting twice around.

Widening the space at the large end. Thus, in Fig. 24, a gear and a cutter are set to have a space widened at the large end e', and the last chip to be cut off by the right side of the cutter, the cutter having been moved to the left, and the blank rotated in the direction of the arrow : in a Universal Milling Machine the same result would be attained by moving the blank to the right and rotating it in the direction of the arrow. It may be well to remember that in setting to finish the side of a tooth, the tooth and the cutter are first separated sidewise, and the blank is then rotated by indexing the spindle to bring the large end of the tooth up against the cutter. This tends

Teeth narrowed more at face than at root. not only to cut the spaces wider at the large pitch circle, but also to cut off still more at the face of the tooth; that is, the teeth may be cut rather thin at the face and left rather thick at the root. This tendency is greater as a cutting angle B O o, Fig. 23, is smaller, or as a bevel gear approaches a spur gear, because when the cutting angle is small the blank must be rotated through a greater arc in order to set to cut the right thickness at the outer pitch circle. This can be understood by Figs. 26 and 27. Fig. 26 is a radial-toothed clutch, which for our present purpose can be regarded as one extreme of a bevel gear in which the teeth are cut square with the axis: the dotted lines indicate the different positions of the cutter, the side of a tooth being finished by the side of the cutter that is on the centre line. In setting to cut these teeth there is the same side adjustment and rotation of the

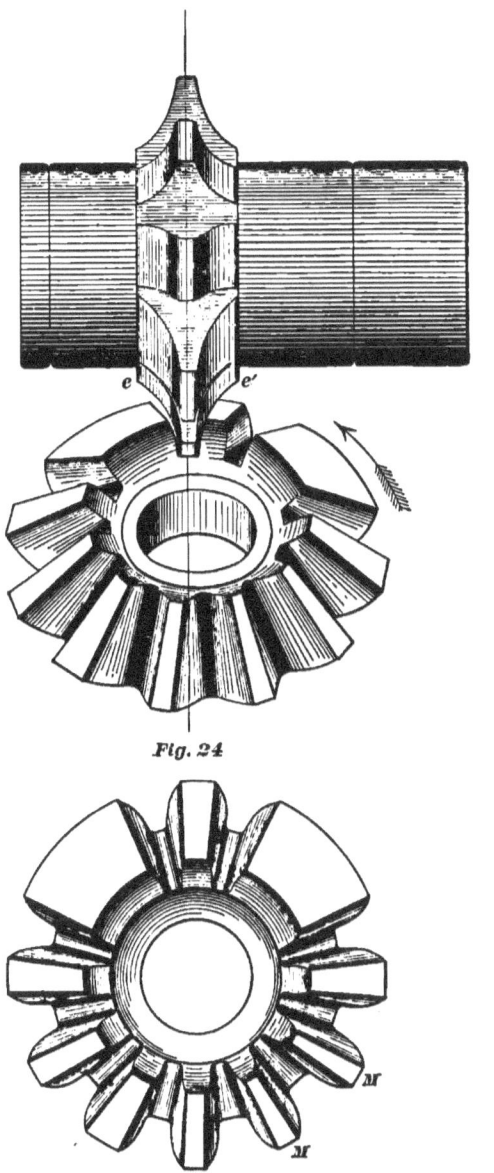

Fig. 24

Fig. 25

spindle as in a bevel gear, but there is no tendency to make a tooth thinner at the face than at the root. On the other hand, if we apply these same adjustments to a spur gear and cutter, Fig. 27, we shall cut the face F much thinner without materially changing the thickness of the root R.

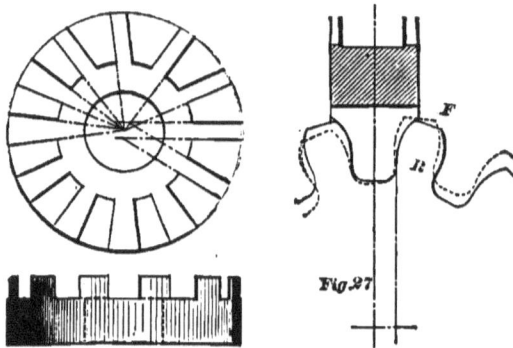

Fig. 26

Almost all bevel gears are between the two extremes of Figs. 26 and 27, so that when the cutting angle B O o, Fig. 28, is smaller than about 30°, this change in the form of the spaces caused by the rotation of the blank may be so great as to necessitate the substitution

Fig. 28

of a cutter that is narrower at c e', Fig. 24, than is called for by the way of figuring that we have just given: thus in our own gear cutting department we might cut the pinion with a No. 6 cutter, instead of a No. 8. The No. 6, being for 17 to 20 teeth, cuts the tooth sides with a longer radius of curvature than the No 8, which may necessitate considerable filing at the small ends of the teeth in order to round them over enough. Fig. 28 shows the same gear as Fig. 25, but in this case the teeth have all been filed similar to M M, Fig. 25.

Different workmen prefer different ways to compromise in the cutting of a bevel gear. When a blank is rotated in adjusting to finish the large end of the teeth there need not be much filing of the small end, if the cutter is right, for a pitch circle of the radius B c, Fig. 23, which for our example is a No. 8 cutter, but the tooth faces may be rather thin at the large ends. This compromise is preferred by nearly all workmen, because it does not require much filing of the teeth: it is the same as is in our catalogue by which we fill any order for bevel gear cutters, unless otherwise specified. This means that we should send a No. 8, 8-pitch bevel gear cutter in reply to an order for a cutter to cut the 12-tooth pinion, Fig. 23; while in our own gear cutting department we might cut the same pinion with a No. 6, 8-pitch cutter, because we prefer to file the teeth at the small end after cutting them to the right thickness at the faces of the large end. We should take a No. 6 instead of a No. 8 only for a 12-tooth pinion that is to run with a gear two or three times as large. We generally step off to the next cutter for pinions fewer than twenty-five teeth, when the number for the teeth has a fraction nearly reaching the range of the next cutter: thus, if twice the line B c in inches, Fig. 23, multiplied by the diametral pitch, equals 20.9, we should use a No. 5 cutter, which is for 21 to 25 teeth inclusive. In filling an order for a gear cutter, we do not consider

Filling the teeth at the small end.

Selection of cutter when teeth are to be filed.

the fraction but send the cutter indicated by the whole number.

Later on we will refer to other compromises that are made in the cutting of bevel gears.

The sizes of the 8-pitch tooth parts, Fig. 23, at the large end, are copied from the table of spur gear teeth, pages 86 to 89.

Form of gear cutting order

The distance Oc' is seven-tenths of the *apex distance* Oc, so that the sizes of the tooth parts at the small end, except f, are seven-tenths the large. The order for cutting these gears goes to the workmen in this form:

LARGE GEAR.

$P = 8$
$N = 24$
$D'' + f = .270''$ $D''' + f = .195''$
$t = .196''$ $t' = .137''$
$s = .125''$ $s' = .087''$
Cutting Angle $= 59° 10'$

SMALL GEAR.

$N = 12$
Cutting Angle $= 22° 18'$

Setting the machine.

Fig. 32 is a side view of a Gear Cutting Machine. A bevel gear blank A is held by the index spindle B. The cutter C is carried by the cutter-slide D. The cutter-slide-carriage E can be set to the cutting angle, the degrees being indicated on the quadrant F.

Fig. 33 is a plan of the machine: in this view the cutter-slide-carriage, in order to show the details a little plainer, is not set to an angle.

Before beginning to cut the cutter is set central with the index spindle and the dial G is set to zero, so that we can adjust the cutter to any required distance out of centre, in either direction. Set the cutter-slide-carriage E, Fig. 32, to the cutting angle of the gear, which for 24-teeth is $59° 10'$; the quadrant being divided to half-degrees, we estimate that 10' or $\frac{1}{6}$ degree more than 59°. Mark the depth of the cut at the outside, as in Fig. 30: it is also well enough to mark the depth at the inside as a check. The thickness of the teeth at the large end is conveniently determined by the solid gauge, Fig. 29. The gear-tooth

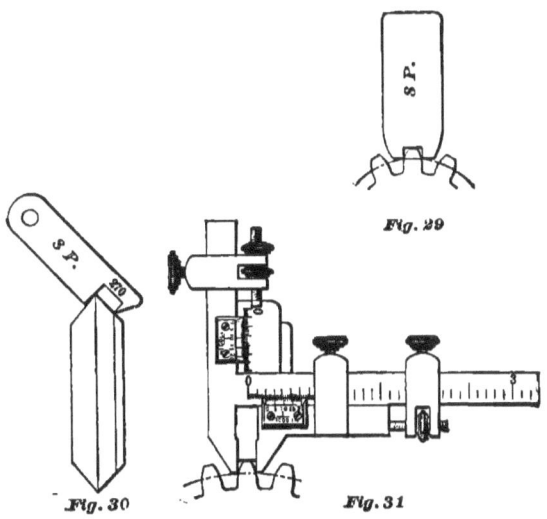

Fig. 29
Fig. 30   Fig. 31

vernier caliper, Fig. 31, will measure the thickness of teeth up to 2 diametral pitch. In the absence of the vernier caliper we can file a gauge, similar to Fig 29, to the thickness of the teeth at the small end.

The index having been set to divide to the right number we cut two spaces central with the blank, leaving a tooth between that is a little too thick, as in the upper part of Fig. 25. If the gear is of cast iron, and the pitch is not coarser than about 5 diametral, this is as far as we go with the central cuts, and we proceed to set the cutter and the blank to finish first one side of the teeth and then the other, going around only twice. The tooth has to be cut away more in proportion from the large than from the small end, which is the reason for setting the cutter out of centre, as in Fig. 24.

Position of side of tooth being finished

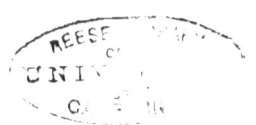

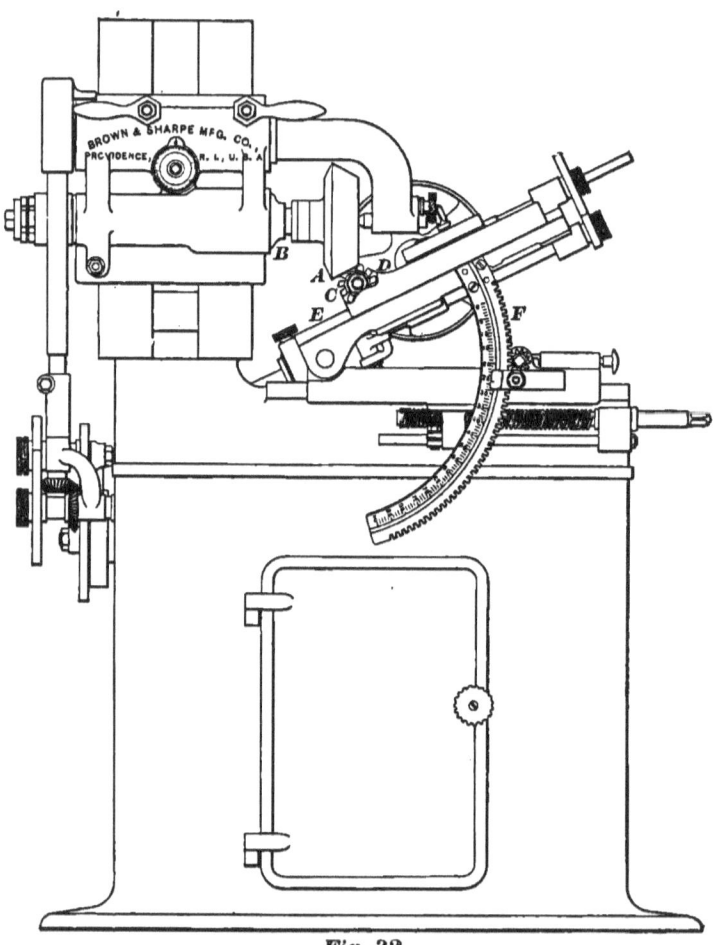

Fig. 32

It is important to remember that the part of the cutter that is finishing one side of a tooth at the pitch line should be central with the gear blank, in order to know at once in which direction to set the cutter out of centre. We can not readily tell how much out of centre to set the cutter until we have cut and tried, because the same part of a cutter does not cut to the pitch line at both ends of a tooth. As a trial distance out of centre we can take about one-tenth to one-eighth of the thickness of the teeth at the large end. The actual distance out of centre for the 12-tooth pinion is .021″; for the 24-tooth gear, .030″, when using cutters listed in our catalogue.

After a little practice a workman can set his blank the trial distance out of centre, and take his first cuts, without any central cuts at all; but it is safer to take central cuts like the upper ones in Fig. 25. The depth of cut is partly controlled by the index-spindle raising-dial-shaft H, Fig. 33, which determines the height of the index spindle, and partly by the position of the cutter spindle. We now set the cutter out of centre the trial distance by means of the cutter-spindle dial-shaft, I, Fig. 33. The trial distance can be about one-tenth the thickness of the tooth at the large end in a 12-tooth pinion, and from that to one-eighth the thickness in a 24-tooth gear and larger. The principle of trimming the teeth more at the large end than at the small is illustrated in Fig. 24, which is to move the cutter away from the tooth to be trimmed, and then to bring the tooth up against the cutter by rotating the blank in the direction of the arrow.

Necessity of central cuts.

Adjustments.

The rotative adjustment of the index spindle is accomplished by loosening the connection between the index worm and the index drive, and turning the worm: the connection is then fastened again. The cutter is now set the same distance out of centre in the other direction, the index spindle is adjusted to trim the other side of the tooth until one end is down nearly to the right thickness. If now the thickness of the small end is in the same proportion to the large end as Oc′ is to Oc, Fig. 23, we can at once adjust to trim the tooth to the right thickness. But if we find that the large end is still going to be too thick when the small end is right, the out of centre must be increased.

It is well to remember this : too much out of centre leaves the small end proportionally too thick, and too little out of centre leaves the small end too thin.

After the proper distance out of centre has been learned the teeth can be finish-cut by going around out of centre first on one side and then on the other without cutting any central spaces at all. The cutter spindle stops, J J, can now be set to control the out of centre of the cutter, without having to adjust by the dial G. If, however, a cast iron gear is 5-pitch or coarser it is usually well to cut central spaces first and then take the two out-of-centre cuts, going around three times in all. Steel gears should be cut three times around.

Blanks are not always turned nearly enough alike to be cut without a different setting for different blanks. If the hubs vary in length the position of the cutter spindle has to be varied. In thus varying, the same depth of cut or the exact $D'' + f$ may not always be reached. A slight difference in the depth is not so objectionable as the incorrect tooth thickness that it may cause. Hence, it is well, after cutting once around and finishing one side of the teeth, to give careful attention to the rotative adjustment of the index spindle so as to cut the right thickness.

After a gear is cut, and before the teeth are filed, it is not always a very satisfactory-looking piece of work. In Fig. 25 the tooth L is as the cutter left it, and is ready to be filed to the shape of the teeth M M, which have been filed. Fig. 34 is the pair of gears that we have been cutting ; the teeth of the 12-tooth pinion have been filed.

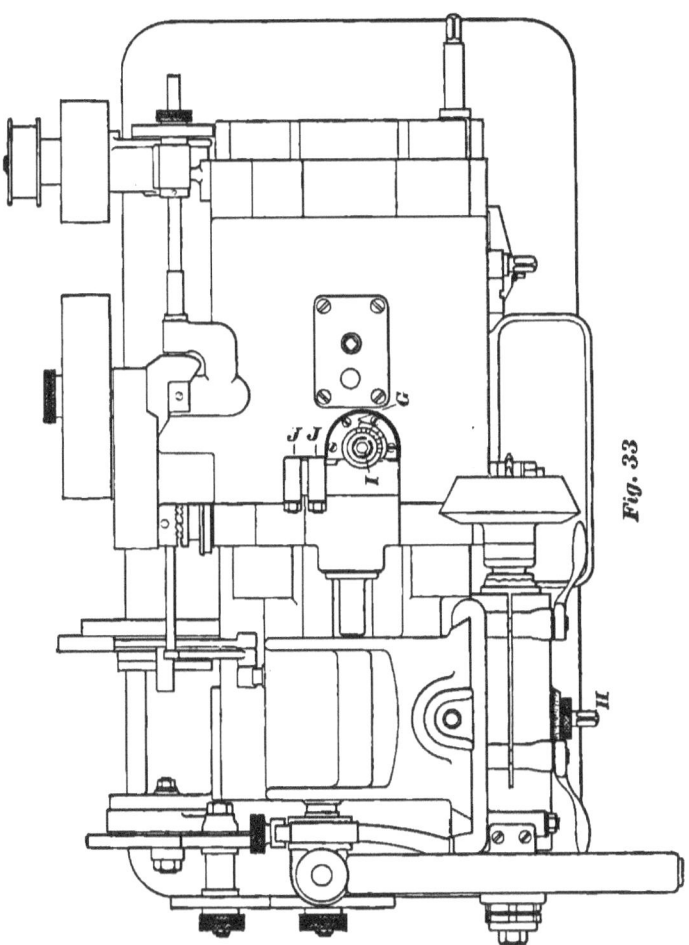

Fig. 33

A second approximation in cutting with a rotary cutter is to widen the spaces at the large end by swinging either the index spindle or the cutter-slide-carriage, so as to pass the cutter through on an angle with the blank side-ways, called the *side-angle*, and not rotate the blank at all to widen the spaces. This side-angle method is employed in our No. 2 Automatic Mitre Gear Cutting Machine: it is available in the manufacture of mitre gears in large quantities, because with the proper relative thickness of cutter, the tooth-thickness comes right by merely adjusting for the side-angle; but for cutting a few gears it is not much liked by workmen, because, in adjusting for the side-angle, the central setting of the cutter is usually lost, and has to be found by guiding into the central slot already cut. If the side-angle mechanism pivots about a line that passes very near the small end of the tooth to be cut, the central setting of the cutter may not be lost. With this method a gear must be cut at least twice around; in widening the spaces at the large end, the teeth are narrowed practically the same amount at the root as at the face, so that this side-angle method requires a wider cutter at e e', Fig. 24, than the first, or rotative method. The amount of filing required to correct the form of the teeth at the small end is about the same as in the first method.

A third approximate method consists in cutting the teeth right at the large end by going around at least twice, and then to trim the teeth at the small end and toward the large with another cutter, going around at least four times in all. This method requires skill and is necessarily a little slow, but it contains possibilities for considerable accuracy.

A fourth method is to have a cutter fully as thick as the spaces at the small end, cut rather deeper than the regular depth at the large end, and go only once around. This is a quick method but more inaccurate than the three preceding: it is available in the manufacture of large numbers of gears when the tooth-face

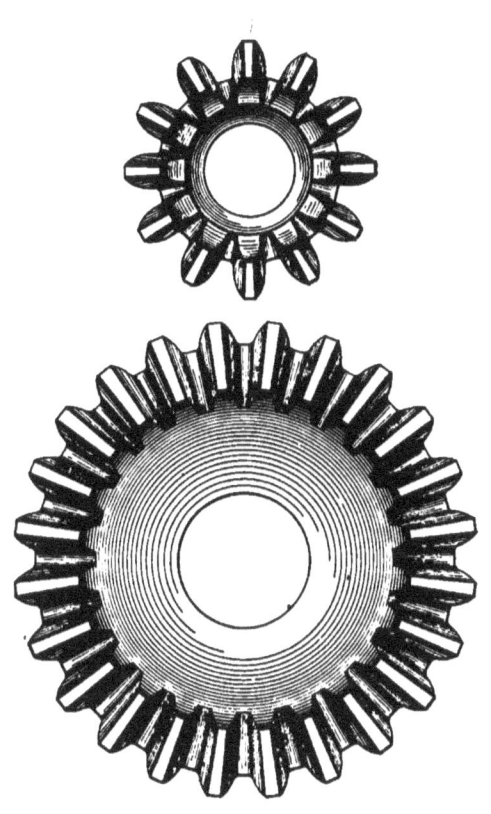

Fig. 34

is short compared with the apex distance. It is little liked, and seldom employed in cutting a few gears : it may require some experimenting to determine the form of cutter. Sometimes the teeth are not cut to the regular depth at the small end in order to have them thick enough, which may necessitate reducing the addendum of the teeth, s', at the small end by turning the blank down. This method is extensively employed by chuck manufacturers.

A machine that cuts bevel gears with a reciprocating motion and using a tool similar to a planer tool is called a Gear Planer and the gears so cut are said to be *planed*.

Planing of bevel gears. One form of Gear Planer is that in which the principle embodied is theoretically correct; this machine originates the tooth curves without a former. Another form of the same class of machines is that in which the tool is guided by a former.

Usually the time consumed in planing a bevel gear is greater than the time necessary to cut the same gear with a rotary cutter, thus proportionately increasing the cost.

Pitches coarser than 4 are more correct and sometimes less expensive when planed; it is hardly practicable, and certainly not economical, to cut a bevel gear as coarse as 3P. with a rotary cutter. In gears as fine as 16P. planing affords no practical gain in quality.

While planing is theoretically correct, yet the wearing of the tool may cause more variation in the thickness of the teeth than the wearing of a rotary cutter, and even a planed gear is sometimes improved by filing.

Mounting of gears. If gears are not correctly mounted in the place where they are to run, they might as well not be planed. In fact, after taking pains in the cutting of any gear, when we come to the mounting of it we should keep right on taking pains.

Angles and sizes of bevel gears. The method of obtaining the sizes and angles pertaining to bevel gears by measuring a drawing is quite convenient, and with care is fairly accurate. Its accuracy depends, of course, upon the careful measuring of a good drawing. We may say, in general, that in measuring a diagram, while we can hardly obtain data mathematically exact, we are not likely to make wild mistakes. Some years ago we depended almost entirely upon measuring, but since the publication of this "Treatise" and our "Formulas in Gearing" we calculate the data without any measuring of a drawing. In the "Formulas in Gearing" there are also tables pertaining to bevel gears.

Several of the cuts and some of the matter in this chapter are taken from an article by O. J. Beale, in the "American Machinist," June 20, 1895.

CUTTERS FOR MITRE AND BEVEL GEARS.

Diametral Pitch.	Diameter of Cutter.	Hole in Cutter.
4	3 3-8″	1 1-4″
5	3 1-16	"
6	2 3-4	1 1-16
8	2 1-2	"
10	2 1-8	7-8
12	2	"
14	2	"
16	1 15-16	"
20	1 7-8	"
24	1 3-4	"

CHAPTER XI.
WORM WHEELS—SIZING BLANKS OF 32 TEETH AND OVER.

Worm.   A WORM is a screw made to mesh with the teeth of a wheel called a *worm-wheel*. As implied at the end of Chapter IV., a section of a worm through its axis is, in outline, the same as a rack of corresponding pitch. This outline can be made either to mesh with single or double curve gear teeth; but worms are usually made for single curve, because, the sides of involute rack teeth being straight (see Chapter IV.), the tool for cutting worm-thread is more easily made. The thread-tool is not usually rounded for giving fillets at bottom of worm-thread.

The rules for circular pitch apply in the size of tooth parts and diameter of pitch-circle of worm-wheel.

Pitch of Worm.   The pitch of a worm or screw is usually given in a way different from the pitch of a gear, viz.: in number of threads to one inch of the length of the worm or screw. Thus, if we say a worm is 2 pitch we mean 2 threads to the inch, or the worm makes two turns to advance the thread one inch. But a worm may be double-threaded, triple-threaded, and so on.

Lead of a Worm-Thread.   To avoid misunderstanding it is better always to call the advance of the worm thread the *lead*. Thus, a worm-thread that advances one inch in one turn we call one-inch *lead* in one turn. A single-thread worm 4 to 1" is ¼" lead. We apply the term pitch to the actual distance between the threads or teeth, as in previous chapters. In single-thread worms the lead and the pitch are alike. If we have to make a worm and wheel so many threads to one inch, we first *divide* 1" *by the number of threads to one inch*, and the quotient *gives us the circular pitch*. Hence, the wheel in Fig. 36 is ½"

Linear Pitch.   circular pitch. The term *linear pitch* expresses ex-

FIG. 35.—WORM AND WORM-WHEEL.
The thread of Worm is left-handed; Worm is single-threaded.

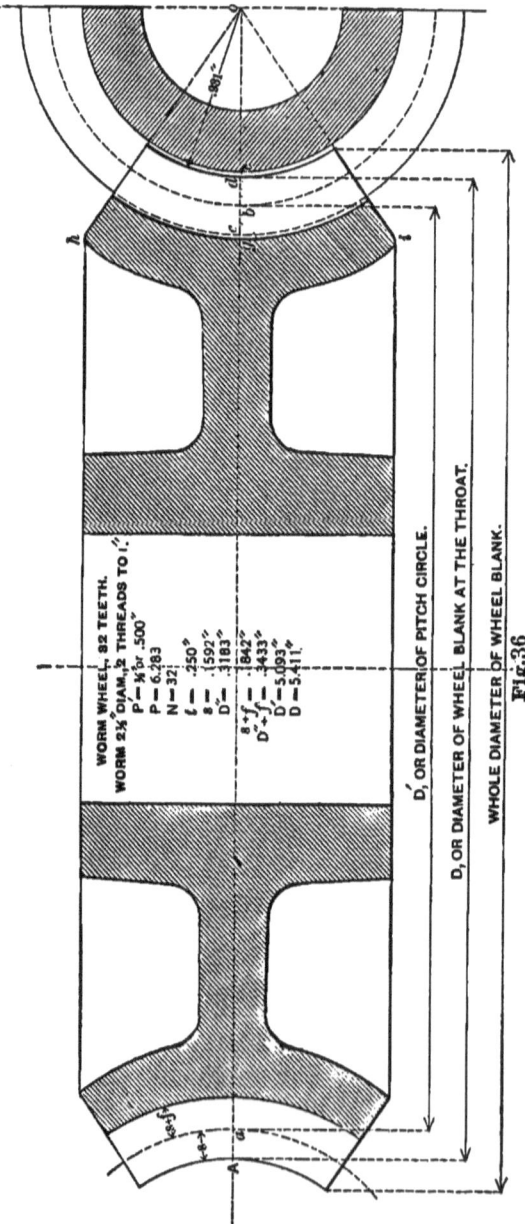

Fig. 36
WORM WHEEL BLANK.

actly what is meant by circular pitch. Linear pitch has the advantage of being an exact use of language when applied to worms and racks. The number of threads to one inch linear, is the reciprocal of the linear pitch.

Multiply 3.1416 by the number of threads to one inch, and the product will be the diametral pitch of the worm-wheel. Thus, we would say of a double-thread worm advancing $1''$ in $1\frac{1}{3}$ turns that:

Lead $=\frac{3}{4}''$ or $.75''$. Linear pitch or $P' = \frac{3}{8}''$ or $.375''$. Diametral pitch or $P = 8.377$. See table of tooth parts.

Drawing of Worm and Worm-wheel.

To make drawing of worm and wheel we obtain data as in circular pitch.

1. Draw center line A O and upon it space off the distance $a\ b$ equal to the diameter of pitch-circle.
2. On each side of these two points lay off the distance s, or the usual addendum $=\frac{1}{P}''$, as $b\ c$ and $b\ d$.
3. From c lay off the distance c O equal to the radius of the worm. The diameter of a worm is generally four or five times the circular pitch.
4. Lay off the distances $c\ g$ and $d\ e$ each equal to f, or the usual clearance at bottom of tooth space.
5. Through c and e draw circles about O. These represent the whole diameter of worm and the diameter at bottom of worm-thread.
6. Draw h O and i O at an angle of $30°$ to $45°$ with A O. These lines give width of face of worm-wheel.
7. Through g and d draw arcs about O, ending in h O and i O.

This operation repeated at a completes the outline of worm-wheel. For 32 teeth and more, the addendum diameter, or D, should be taken at the throat or smallest diameter of wheel, as in Fig. 36. *Measure sketch for whole diameter of wheel-blank.*

The foregoing instructions and sketch are for cases where the teeth of the wheels are finished with a *hob*.

Teeth of Wheels finished with Hob.

A HOB is shown in Fig. 37, being a steel piece threaded with the same tool that threads the worm, then grooved to make teeth for cutting, and hardened.

Hob.

The whole diameter of hob should be at least $2\ f$, or twice the clearance larger than the worm.

Proportions of Hob.

In our relieved hobs the diameter is made still larger in order to give the proper clearance. The outer corners of hob-thread can be rounded down as far as the clearance distance. The width at top of the hob-thread before rounding should be .31 of the linear, or circular pitch $=.31P'$. The whole depth of thread should be the ordinary working depth plus the clearance $= D''+f$. The diameter at bottom of hob-thread should be $2f$ larger than the diameter at bottom of worm-thread. For thread-tool and worm-thread see end of Chapter IV. The thickness of cutter for grooving small hobs, say less than two inches diameter, can be about $\frac{1}{2}$ the width of thread at top plus $\frac{1}{8}''=.\frac{3\ 3\ 5}{2}P'+\frac{1}{8}''$. The width of lands at the bottom

FIG. 37.—HOB.

can be about the depth of thread plus $\frac{1}{8}''=D''+2f+\frac{1}{8}''$. The grooves are usually cut with a round edge cutter, the parallel part of cutter just reaching the bottom of thread, making the half-round bottom of grooves below the bottom of thread. In small hobs, the teeth are often not relieved between the grooves. In large hobs or those more than three inches diameter, the teeth may be cut with radial faces, cutting the space wider at the outer part so as to leave the faces and backs of teeth about parallel, and the teeth should be relieved. This can be done in our Universal Milling Machine. A common way in hobs two to three inches in diameter, is to relieve with a file.

The teeth of the wheel are first cut as nearly to the finished form as practicable; the hob and worm-wheel are mounted upon shafts and hob placed in mesh as in Fig. 35. . The hob is now made to rotate, and is dropped deeper into the wheel at each revolution of the wheel until teeth are finished. The hob generally drives the worm-wheel during this operation. The Universal Milling Machine is very convenient for doing this work, and with it the distance between axes of worm and wheel can be readily noted. We have machines for hobbing wheels, in which the work spindle is driven by gearing so that the hob does not have to do the work of driving the wheel. The object of hobbing a wheel is to get more bearing surface of the teeth upon worm-thread. The worm-wheels, Figs. 35 and 43, were hobbed. By hobbing we produce outline of teeth something like the thread of a nut. *How to use the Hob.* *Universal Milling Machine used in Hobbing.* *Why a Wheel is Hobbed.*

If we make the diameter of a worm-wheel blank, that is to have less than 30 teeth, by the common rules for sizing blanks, and finish the teeth with a hob, we shall find the flanks of teeth near the bottom to be *undercut* or hollowing. This is caused by the interference spoken of in Chapter VI. Thirty teeth was there given as a limit, which will be right when teeth are made to circle arcs. With pressure angle $75\frac{1}{2}°$, and rack-teeth with usual addendum, this interference of rack-teeth with flanks of gear-teeth commences at 31 teeth ($31\frac{7}{10}$ geometrically), and interferes with nearly the whole flank in wheel of 12 teeth. *Worm-Wheel Blanks with Less than 30 Teeth.* *Interference of Thread and Flank.*

In Fig 38 the blank for worm-wheel of 12 teeth was sized by the same rule as given for Fig. 36. The wheel and worm are sectioned to show shape of teeth at the mid-plane of wheel. The flanks of teeth are undercut by the hob. The worm-thread does not have a good bearing on flanks inside of A, the bearing being that of a corner against a surface. *Fig. 38.*

In Fig 39 the blank for wheel was sized so that pitch-circle comes midway between outermost part of teeth and innermost point obtained by worm thread. *Fig. 39.*

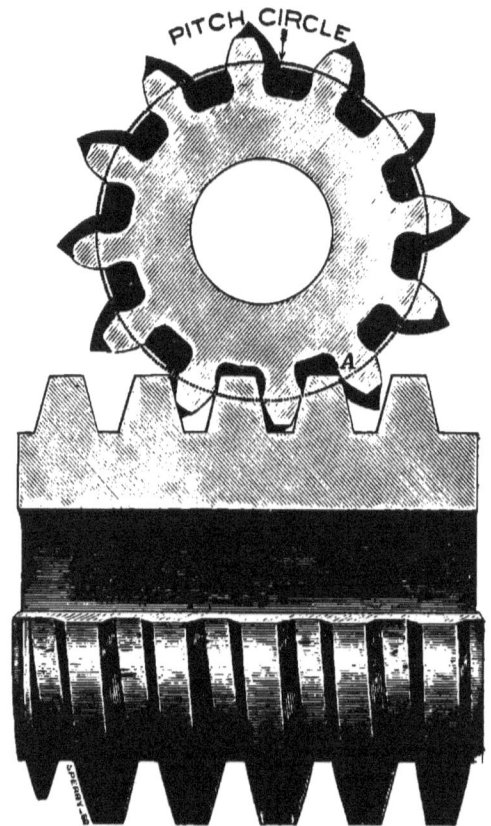

Fig. 38.

Fig. 30.

This rule for sizing worm-wheel blanks has been in use to some extent. The hob has cut away flanks of teeth still more than in Fig. 38. The pitch circle in Fig. 39 is the same diameter as the pitch-circle in Fig. 38. The same hob was used for both wheels. The flanks in this wheel are so much undercut as to materially lessen the bearing surface of teeth and worm-thread.

Interference Avoided. In Chapter VI. the interference of teeth in high-numbered gears and racks with flanks of 12 teeth was remedied by rounding off the addenda. Although it would be more systematic to round off the threads of a worm, making them, like rack-teeth, to mesh with interchangeable gears, yet this has not generally been done, because it is easier to make a worm-thread tool with straight sides.

Instead of cutting away the addenda of worm-thread, we can avoid the interference with flanks of wheels having less than 30 teeth by making wheel blanks larger.

Fig. 40. The flanks of wheel in Fig. 40 are not undercut, because the diameter of wheel is so large that there is hardly any tooth inside the pitch-circle. The pitch-circle in Fig. 40 is the same size as pitch-circles in Figs. 38 and 39. This wheel was sized *Diameter at Throat to Avoid Interference.* by the following rule: Multiply the *pitch diameter* of the wheel by .937, and add to the product four times the addendum (4 s); the sum will be the diameter for the blank at the throat or small part. To get the whole diameter, make a sketch with diameter of throat to the foregoing rule and measure the sketch.

It is impractical to hob a wheel of 12 to about 16 or 18 teeth when blank is sized by this rule, unless the wheel is driven by independent mechanism and not by the hob. The diameter across the outermost parts of teeth, as at A B, is considerably less than the largest diameter of wheel before it was hobbed.

In general it is well to size all blanks, as by page 63 and Figs. 36 and 38, when the wheels are to be hobbed. Of course, if the wheel is to be hobbed the

Fig. 40.

cutter should be thin enough to leave stock for finishing. The spaces can be cut the full depth, the cutter being dropped in.

To get angle of worm-thread, it is best to apply protractor directly to the thread, as computing the angle affords but little help. Set gear cutter-head as near the angle as can be seen from trial with protractor upon thread; cut a few teeth; try in worm. Generally the cutter-head has to be changed before the worm will take the right position.

Blank Like a Spur-Wheel. When worm-wheels are not hobbed it is better to turn blanks like a spur-wheel. Little is gained by having wheels curved to fit worm unless teeth are finished with a hob. The teeth can be cut in a straight path diagonally across face of blank, to fit angle of worm-thread, as in Figs. 41 and 44.

Wheels for Gear-Cutting Machines. For dividing wheels to gear-cutting engines the blanks are turned like a spur-wheel and a cutter about $\frac{1}{16}''$ larger diameter than the worm, is dropped in, as in Figs. 42 and 45, and the worm-thread is slightly rounded at the outer corners. The radius for rounding thread can be $\frac{1}{4}$ the width of thread at the top.

Some mechanics prefer to make dividing wheels in two parts, joined in a plane perpendicular to axis, hob teeth; then turn one part round upon the other, match teeth and fasten parts together in the new position, and hob again with a view to eliminate errors.

With an accurate cutting engine we have found wheels like Figs. 42 and 45, not hobbed, every way satisfactory. Dividing wheels of 2 feet diameter and less are generally made without arms, the part between hub and rim being a solid web. As to the different

Figures 43, 44 and 45. wheels, Figs. 43, 44 and 45, when worm is in right position at the start, the life-time of Fig. 43, under heavy and continuous work, will be the longest.

Fig. 44 can be run in mesh with a gear or a rack as well as with a worm when made within the angular limits commonly required. Strictly, neither two gears made in this way, nor a gear and a rack would be mathematically exact as they might bear on the sides of the gear or at the ends of the teeth only and not in the middle. At the start the con-

Fig. 41.

Worm-wheel with teeth cut in a straight path diagonally across face. Worm is double-threaded.

Fig. 42.
Worm and Worm-Wheel, for Gear-cutting Engine.

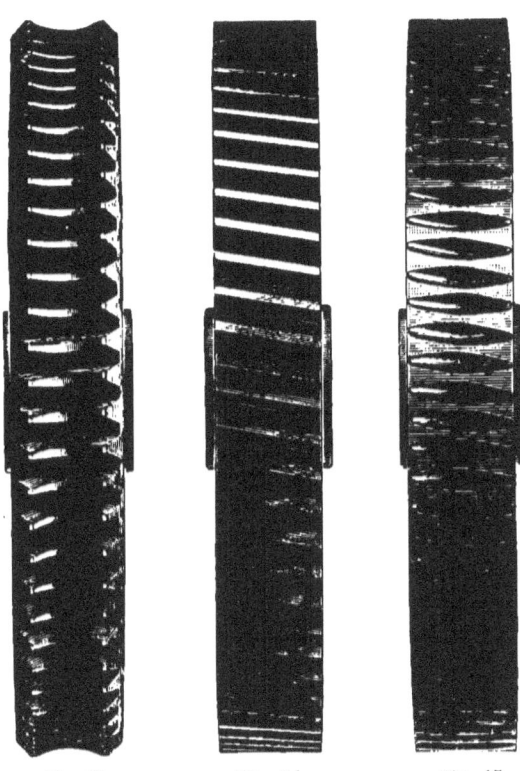

Fig. 43.   *Fig. 44.*   *Fig. 45.*

tact of teeth in this wheel upon worm-thread is in points only: yet such wheels have been many years successfully used in elevators.

Fig. 45 is a neat-looking wheel. In gear cutting engines where the workman has occasion to turn the work spindle by hand, it is not so rough to take hold of as Figs. 43 and 44. The teeth are less liable to injury than the teeth of Figs. 43 and 44.

Some designers prefer to take off the outermost part of teeth in wheels (Figs. 35 and 43), as shown in these two figures, and not leave them sharp, as in Fig. 19.

We do not know that this serves any purpose except a matter of looks.

In ordering worms and worm wheels the centre distances should be given.

If there can be any limit allowed in the centre distance it should be so stated.

For instance, the distance from the centre of a worm to the centre of a worm wheel might be calculated at 6" but 5 31-32" or 6 1-32" might answer.

By stating all the limits that can be allowed, there may be a saving in the cost of work because time need not be wasted in trying to make work within narrow limits than need be.

HOBS WITH RELIEVED TEETH.

We are prepared to make hobs of any size with the teeth relieved the same as our gear cutters. The teeth can be ground on their faces without changing their form. The hobs are made with a precision screw so that the pitch of the thread is accurate before hardening.

CHAPTER XII.

SIZING GEARS WHEN THE DISTANCE BETWEEN CENTRES AND THE RATIOS OF SPEEDS ARE FIXED—GENERAL REMARKS—WIDTH OF FACE OF SPUR GEARS—SPEED OF GEAR CUTTERS—TABLE OF TOOTH PARTS.

Let us suppose that we have two shafts 14" apart, center to center, and wish to connect them by gears so that they will have speed ratio 6 to 1. We add the 6 and 1 together, and divide 14" by the sum and get 2" for a quotient; this 2", multiplied by 6, gives us the radius of pitch circle of large wheel = 12". In the same manner we get 2" as radius of pitch circle of small wheel. Doubling the radius of each gear, we obtain 24" and 4" as the pitch diameters of the two wheels. The two numbers that form a ratio are called the terms of the ratio. We have now the rule for obtaining pitch-circle diameter of two wheels of a given ratio to connect shafts a given distance apart: *[Center distance and Ratio fixed.]*

Divide the center distance by the sum of the terms of the ratio; find the product of twice the quotient by each term separately, and the two products will be the pitch diameters of the two wheels. *[Rule for Diameter of Pitch Circles.]*

It is well to give special attention to learning the rules for sizing blanks and teeth; these are much oftener needed than the method of forming tooth outlines.

A blank 1¼" diameter is to have 16 teeth: what will the pitch be? What will be the diameter of the pitch circle? See Chapter V.

A good practice will be to compute a table of tooth parts. The work can be compared with the tables pages 86–89.

In computing it is well to take π to more than four places, π to nine places = 3.141592653. $\frac{1}{\pi}$ to nine places = .318309886.

There is no such thing as pure rolling contact in teeth of wheels; they always rub, and, in time, will wear themselves out of shape and may become noisy.

Bevel gears, when correctly formed, run smoother than spur gears of same diameter and pitch, because the teeth continue in contact longer than the teeth of spur gears. For this reason annular gears run smoother than either bevel or spur gears.

Sometimes gears have to be cut a little deeper than designed, in order to run easily on their shafts. If any departure is made in ratio of pitch diameters it is better to have the driving gear the larger, that is, cut the follower smaller. For wheels coarser than eight diametral pitch (8 P), it is generally better to cut twice around, when accurate work is wanted, also for large wheels, as the expansion of parts from heat often causes inaccurate work when cut but once around. There is not so much trouble from heat in plain or web gears as in arm gears.

Width of Spur Gear faces. The width of cast-iron gear faces for general purposes can be made to the following rule:

Divide 8 by the diametral pitch and add $\frac{1}{4}''$ to the quotient; the sum will be width of face for the pitch required.

Example: What width of face for gear 4 P? Dividing 8 by 4 and adding $\frac{1}{4}''$ we obtain $2\frac{1}{4}''$, for width of face. For change gears on lathes, where it is desirable not to have face very wide, the following rule can be used:

Divide 4 by the diametral pitch and add $\frac{1}{2}''$.

By the latter rule a 4 P change gear would have but $1\frac{1}{2}''$ face.

Speed of Gear Cutters. The speed of gear cutters is subject to so many conditions that definite rules cannot be given. We append a table of average speeds. A coarse pitch cutter for pinion, 12 teeth, would usually be run slower than a cutter for a large gear of same pitch.

TABLE OF AVERAGE SPEEDS FOR GEAR-CUTTERS.

Diametral Pitch of Cutter.	Diameter of Cutter.	Turns per minute cutting Cast Iron.	Turns per minute cutting Wrought Iron and Steel.	Feed to One Turn of Cutter in Cast Iron.	Feed to One Turn of Cutter in Wrought Iron and Steel.	Feed per minute in Cast Iron.	Feed per minute in Wrought Iron and Steel.
2	5 in.	24	18	.025 in.	.011 in.	.60 in.	.20 in.
2½	4¼ "	30	24	.028 "	.013 "	.84 "	.31 "
3	3 13/16 "	36	28	.031 "	.015 "	1.12 "	.42 "
4	3⅜ "	42	32	.034 "	.017 "	1.43 "	.54 "
5	3 1/10 "	50	40	.037 "	.019 "	1.85 "	.76 "
6	2 11/16 "	75	55	.030 "	.016 "	2.25 "	.88 "
7	2 9/16 "	85	65	.032 "	.018 "	2.72 "	1.17 "
8	2½ "	95	75	.034 "	.020 "	3.23 "	1.50 "
10	2⅜ "	125	90	.026 "	.014 "	3.25 "	1.26 "
12	2 "	135	100	.027 "	.017 "	3.64 "	1.70 "
20	1⅞ "	145	115	.029 "	.021 "	4.20 "	2.41 "
32	1¾ "	160	135	.031 "	.025 "	4.96 "	3.37 "

In brass the speed of gear-cutters can be twice as fast as in cast iron. Clock-makers and those making a specialty of brass gears exceed this rate even. A 12 P cutter has been run 1,200 (twelve hundred) turns a minute in bronze. A 32 P cutter has been run 7,000 (seven thousand) turns a minute in soft brass. *Speed in Brass.*

In cutting 5 P cast-iron gears, 75 teeth, a No. 1, 6 P cutter was run 136 (one hundred and thirty-six) turns a minute, roughing the spaces out the full 5 P depth; the teeth were then finished with a 5 P cutter, running 208 (two hundred and eight) turns a minute, feeding by hand. The cutter stood well, but, of course, the cast iron was quite soft. A 4 P cutter has finished teeth at one cut, in cast-iron gears, 86 teeth, running 48 (forty-eight) turns a minute and feeding $\frac{1}{16}$" at one turn, or 3 in. in a minute. *Examples from Practice.*

Hence, while it is generally safe to run cutters as in the table, yet when many gears are to be cut it is well to see if cutters will stand a higher speed and more feed.

In gears coarser than 4 P it is more economical to first cut the full depth with a stocking cutter and then finish with a gear cutter. This stocking cutter is made on the principle of a circular splitting saw for wood. The teeth, however, are not set; but side relief is obtained by making sides of cutter blank hollowing. The shape of stocking cutter can be same as bottom of spaces in a 12-tooth gear, and the thickness of cutter can be $\frac{1}{5}$ of the circular pitch, see page 40.

Keep Cutters sharp. The matter of keeping cutters sharp is so important that it has sometimes been found best to have the workman grind them at stated times, and not wait until he can see that the cutters are dull. Thus, have him grind every two hours or after cutting a stated number of gears. Cutters of the style that can be ground upon their tooth faces without changing form are rapidly destroyed if allowed to run after they are dull. Cutters are oftener wasted by trying to cut with them when they are dull than by too much grinding. Grind the faces radial with a free cutting wheel. Do not let the wheel become glazed, as this will draw the temper of the cutter.

In Chapter VI. was given a series of cutters for cutting gears having 12 teeth and more. Thus, it was there implied that any gear of same pitch, having 135 teeth, 136 teeth, and so on up to the largest gears, and, also, a rack, could be cut with one cutter. If this cutter is 4 P, we would cut with it all 4 P gears, having 135 teeth or more, and we would also cut with it a 4 P rack. Now, instead of always referring to a cutter by the number of teeth in gears it is designed to cut, it has been found convenient to designate it by a letter or by a number. Thus, we call a cutter of 4 P, made to cut gears 135 teeth to a rack, inclusive, No. 1, 4 P.

We have adopted numbers for designating involute
Involute Gear Cutters. gear-cutters as in the following table:

No. 1 will cut wheels from 135 teeth to a rack inclusive.
" 2 "   "   55 "   134 teeth "
" 3 "   "   35 "   54 "   "
" 4 "   "   26 "   34 "   "
" 5 "   "   21 "   25 "   "
" 6 "   "   17 "   20 "   "
" 7 "   "   14 "   16 "   "
" 8 "   "   12 "   13 "   "

By this plan it takes eight cutters to cut all gears having twelve teeth and over, of any one pitch.

Thus it takes eight cutters to cut all involute 4 P gears having twelve teeth and more. It takes eight other cutters to cut all involute gears of 5 P, having 12 teeth and more. A No. 8, 5 P cutter cuts only 5 P gears having 12 and 13 teeth. A No. 6, 10 P cutter cuts only 10 P gears having 17, 18, 19 and 20 teeth. On each cutter is stamped the number of teeth at the limits of its range, as well as the number of the cutter. The number of the cutter relates only to the number of teeth in gears that the cutter is made for.

In ordering cutters for involute spur-gears two things must be given:

1. *Either the number of teeth to be cut in the gear or the number of the cutter, as given in the foregoing table.*   How to order Involute Cutters.

2. *Either the pitch of the gear or the diameter and number of teeth to be cut in the gear.*

If 25 teeth are to be cut in a 6 P involute gear, the cutter will be No. 5, 6 P, which cuts all 6 P gears from 21 to 25 teeth inclusive. If it is desired to cut gears from 15 to 25 teeth, three cutters will be needed, No. 5, No. 6 and No. 7 of the pitch required. If the pitch is 8 and gears 15 to 25 teeth are to be cut, the cutters should be No. 5, 8 P, No. 6, 8 P, and No. 7, 8 P.

For each pitch of epicycloidal, or double-curve gears, 24 cutters are made. In coarse-pitch gears, the variation in the shape of spaces between gears of consecutive-numbered teeth is greater than in fine-pitch gears. A set of cutters for each pitch, to consist of so large a number as 24, has been established because double curve teeth have generally been preferred in coarse-pitch gears, though the tendency of late years is toward the involute form.   Epicycloidal or Double-curve Cutters.

Our double curve cutters have a guide shoulder on each side for the depth to cut. When this shoulder just reaches the periphery of the blank the depth is right. The marks which these shoulders make on the blank, should be as narrow as can be seen, when the blanks are sized right.

Double-curve gear-cutters are designated by letters instead of by numbers; this is to avoid confusion in ordering.

Following is the list of epicycloidal or double-curve gear-cutters:—

Table of Epicycloidal or Double-curve Gear Cutters.

Cutter A cuts 12 teeth.	Cutter M cuts 27 to 29 teeth.
" B " 13 "	" N " 30 " 33 "
" C " 14 "	" O " 34 " 37 "
" D " 15 "	" P " 38 " 42 "
" E " 16 "	" Q " 43 " 49 "
" F " 17 "	" R " 50 " 59 "
" G " 18 "	" S " 60 " 74 "
" H " 19 "	" T " 75 " 99 "
" I " 20 "	" U " 100 " 149 "
" J " 21 to 22	" V " 150 " 249 "
" K " 23 to 24	" W " 250 " Rack.
" L " 24 to 26	" X " Rack.

A cutter that cuts more than one gear is made of proper form for the smallest gear in its range. Thus, cutter J for 21 to 22 teeth is correct for 21 teeth; cutter S for 60 to 74 teeth is correct for 60 teeth, and so on.

How to order Epicycloidal Cutters. In ordering epicycloidal gear-cutters designate the letter of the cutter as in the foregoing table, also either give the pitch or give data that will enable us to determine the pitch, the same as directed for involute cutters.

More care is required in making and adjusting epicycloidal gears than in making involute gears.

How to order Bevel Gear Cutters. In ordering bevel gear cutters three things must be given:

1. *The number of teeth in each gear.*
2. *Either the pitch of gears or the largest pitch diameter of each gear; see Fig.* 17.
3. *The length of tooth face.*

If the shafts are not to run at right angles, it should be so stated, and the angle given. Involute cutters only are used for cutting bevel gears. No attempt should be made to cut epicyclodial tooth bevel gears with rotary disk cutters.

In ordering worm-wheel cutters, three things must be given: *How to order Worm-gear Cutters.*
1. *Number of teeth in the wheel.*
2. *Pitch of the worm; see Chapter XI.*
3. *Whole diameter of worm.*

In any order connected with gears or gear-cutters, when the word "Diameter" occurs, we usually understand that the *pitch diameter* is meant. When the *whole* diameter of a gear is meant it should be plainly written. Care in giving an order often saves the delay of asking further instructions. An order for one gear-cutter to cut from 25 to 30 teeth cannot be filled, because it takes two cutters of involute form to cut from 25 to 30 teeth, and three cutters of epicycloidal form to cut from 25 to 30 teeth.

Sheet zinc is convenient to sketch gears upon, and also for making templets. Before making sketch, it is well to give the zinc a dark coating with the following mixture: Dissolve 1 ounce of sulphate of copper (blue vitriol) in about 4 ounces of water, and add about one-half teaspoonful of nitric acid. Apply a thin coating with a piece of waste.

This mixture will give a thin coating of copper to iron or steel, but the work should then be rubbed dry. Care should be taken not to leave the mixture where it is not wanted, as it rusts iron and steel.

We have sometimes been asked why gears are noisy. Not many questions can be asked us to which we can give a less definite answer than to the question why gears are noisy.

We can indicate only some of the causes which may make gears noisy, such as :—depth of cutting not right—in this particular gears are oftener cut too deep than not deep enough; cutting not central—this may make gears noisy in one direction when they are quiet while running in the other direction; centre distance not right—if too deep the outer corners of the teeth in one gear may strike the fillets of the teeth in the other gear; shafts not parallel; frame of the machine of such a form as to give off sound vibrations. Even when we examine a pair of gears we cannot always tell what is the matter.

NOTE.—For any pitch not in the following tables to find corresponding part:—multiply the tabular value for one inch by the circular pitch required, and the product will be the value for the pitch given. Example: What is the value of s for 4 inch circular pitch? .3183=s for 1" P' and .3183 × 4 = 1.2732=s for 4" P'.

NOTE.—For an explanation of the expression $\frac{1''}{P'}$, see page 17.

The expression "Addendum and 1-P'" (addendum and a diameter pitch) means the distance of a tooth outside of pitch line and also the distance occupied for every tooth upon the diameter of pitch circle.

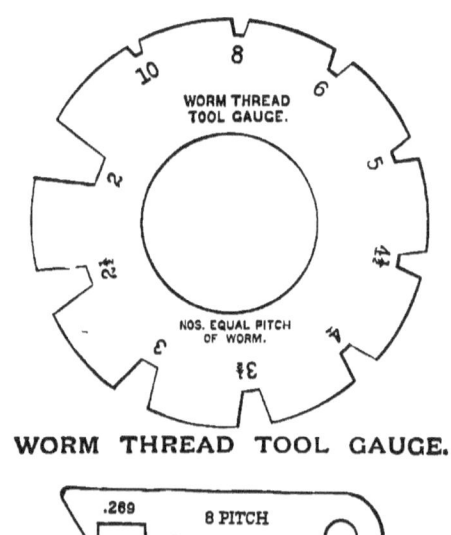

WORM THREAD TOOL GAUGE.

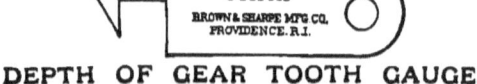

DEPTH OF GEAR TOOTH GAUGE.

GEAR CUTTERS.

GEAR WHEELS.

TABLE OF TOOTH PARTS—CIRCULAR PITCH IN FIRST COLUMN.

Circular Pitch.	Threads or Teeth per inch Linear.	Diametral Pitch.	Thickness of Tooth on Pitch Line.	Addendum and $\frac{1''}{P}$.	Working Depth of Tooth.	Depth of Space below Pitch Line.	Whole Depth of Tooth.	Width of Thread-Tool at End.	Width of Thread at Top.
P'	$\frac{1''}{P'}$	P	t	s	D''	$s+f$	$D''+f$	$P'\times.31$	$P'\times.335$
2	$\frac{1}{2}$	1.5708	1.0000	.6366	1.2732	.7366	1.3732	.6200	.6700
$1\frac{7}{8}$	$\frac{8}{15}$	1.6755	.9375	.5968	1.1937	.6906	1.2874	.5813	.6281
$1\frac{3}{4}$	$\frac{4}{7}$	1.7952	.8750	.5570	1.1141	.6445	1.2016	.5425	.5863
$1\frac{5}{8}$	$\frac{8}{13}$	1.9333	.8125	.5173	1.0345	.5985	1.1158	.5038	.5444
$1\frac{1}{2}$	$\frac{2}{3}$	2.0944	.7500	.4775	.9549	.5525	1.0299	.4650	.5025
$1\frac{7}{16}$	$\frac{16}{23}$	2.1855	.7187	.4576	.9151	.5294	.9870	.4456	.4816
$1\frac{3}{8}$	$\frac{8}{11}$	2.2848	.6875	.4377	.8754	.5064	.9441	.4262	.4606
$1\frac{5}{16}$	$\frac{16}{21}$	2.3936	.6562	.4178	.8356	.4834	.9012	.4069	.4397
$1\frac{1}{4}$	$\frac{4}{5}$	2.5133	.6250	.3979	.7958	.4604	.8583	.3875	.4188
$1\frac{3}{16}$	$\frac{16}{19}$	2.6456	.5937	.3780	.7560	.4374	.8156	.3681	.3978
$1\frac{1}{8}$	$\frac{8}{9}$	2.7925	.5625	.3581	.7162	.4143	.7724	.3488	3769
$1\frac{1}{16}$	$\frac{16}{17}$	2.9568	.5312	.3382	.6764	.3913	.7295	.3294	.3559
1	1	3.1416	.5000	.3183	.6366	.3683	.6866	.3100	.3350
$\frac{15}{16}$	$1\frac{1}{15}$	3.3510	.4687	.2984	.5968	.3453	.6437	.2906	.3141
$\frac{7}{8}$	$1\frac{1}{7}$	3.5904	.4375	.2785	.5570	.3223	.6007	.2713	.2931
$\frac{13}{16}$	$1\frac{3}{13}$	3.8666	.4062	.2586	.5173	.2993	.5579	.2519	.2722
$\frac{3}{4}$	$1\frac{1}{3}$	4.1888	.3750	.2387	.4775	.2762	.5150	.2325	.2513
$\frac{11}{16}$	$1\frac{5}{11}$	4.5696	.3437	.2189	.4377	.2532	.4720	.2131	.2303
$\frac{2}{3}$	$1\frac{1}{2}$	4.7124	.3333	.2122	.4244	.2455	.4577	.2066	.2233

TABLE OF TOOTH PARTS.—Continued.

CIRCULAR PITCH IN FIRST COLUMN.

Circular Pitch.	Threads or Teeth per inch Linear.	Diametral Pitch.	Thickness of Tooth on Pitch Line.	Addendum and $\frac{1''}{P}$	Working Depth of Tooth.	Depth of Space below Pitch Line.	Whole Depth of Tooth.	Width of Thread-Tool at End.	Width of Thread at Top.
P'	$\frac{1''}{P'}$	P	t	"	D"	s+f	D"+f	P'×.31	P'×.335
$\frac{5}{8}$	$1\frac{3}{5}$	5.0265	.3125	.1989	.3979	.2301	.4291	.1938	.2094
$\frac{9}{16}$	$1\frac{7}{9}$	5.5851	.2812	.1790	.3581	.2071	.3862	.1744	.1884
$\frac{1}{2}$	2	6.2832	.2500	.1592	.3183	.1842	.3433	.1550	.1675
$\frac{7}{16}$	$2\frac{2}{7}$	7.1808	.2187	.1393	.2785	.1611	.3003	.1356	.1466
$\frac{2}{5}$	$2\frac{1}{2}$	7.8540	.2000	.1273	.2546	.1473	.2746	.1240	.1340
$\frac{3}{8}$	$2\frac{2}{3}$	8.3776	.1875	.1194	.2387	.1381	.2575	.1163	.1256
$\frac{1}{3}$	3	9.4248	.1666	.1061	.2122	.1228	.2289	.1033	.1117
$\frac{5}{16}$	$3\frac{1}{5}$	10.0531	.1562	.0995	.1989	.1151	.2146	.0969	.1047
$\frac{2}{7}$	$3\frac{1}{2}$	10.9956	.1429	.0909	.1819	.1052	.1962	.0886	.0957
$\frac{1}{4}$	4	12.5664	.1250	.0796	.1591	.0921	.1716	.0775	.0838
$\frac{2}{9}$	$4\frac{1}{2}$	14.1372	.1111	.0707	.1415	.0818	.1526	.0689	.0744
$\frac{1}{5}$	5	15.7080	.1000	.0637	.1273	.0737	.1373	.0620	.0670
$\frac{3}{16}$	$5\frac{1}{3}$	16.7552	.0937	.0597	.1194	.0690	.1287	.0581	.0628
$\frac{1}{6}$	6	18.8496	.0833	.0531	.1061	.0614	.1144	.0517	.0558
$\frac{1}{7}$	7	21.9911	.0714	.0455	.0910	.0526	.0981	.0443	.0479
$\frac{1}{8}$	8	25.1327	.0625	.0398	.0796	.0460	.0858	.0388	.0419
$\frac{1}{9}$	9	28.2743	.0555	.0354	.0707	.0409	.0763	.0344	.0372
$\frac{1}{10}$	10	31.4159	.0500	.0318	.0637	.0368	.0687	.0310	.0335
$\frac{1}{16}$	16	50.2655	.0312	.0199	.0398	.0230	.0429	.0194	.0209

GEAR WHEELS.

TABLE OF TOOTH PARTS—DIAMETRAL PITCH IN FIRST COLUMN.

Diametral Pitch.	Circular Pitch.	Thickness of Tooth on Pitch Line.	Addendum and $\frac{1''}{p}$	Working Depth of Tooth.	Depth of Space below Pitch Line.	Whole Depth of Tooth.
P	P'	t	s	D'	s+f.	D''+f.
½	6.2832	3.1416	2.0000	4.0000	2.3142	4.3142
¾	4.1888	2.0944	1.3333	2.6666	1.5428	2.8761
1	3.1416	1.5708	1.0000	2.0000	1.1571	2.1571
1¼	2.5133	1.2566	.8000	1.6000	.9257	1.7257
1½	2.0944	1.0472	.6666	1.3333	.7714	1.4381
1¾	1.7952	.8976	.5714	1 1429	.6612	1.2326
2	1.5708	.7854	.5000	1.0000	.5785	1.0785
2¼	1.3963	.6981	.4444	.8888	.5143	.9587
2½	1.2566	.6283	.4000	.8000	.4628	.8628
2¾	1.1424	.5712	.3636	.7273	.4208	.7844
3	1.0472	.5236	.3333	.6666	.3857	.7190
3½	.8976	.4488	.2857	.5714	.3306	.6163
4	.7854	.3927	.2500	.5000	.2893	.5393
5	.6283	.3142	.2000	.4000	.2314	.4314
6	.5236	.2618	.1666	.3333	.1928	.3595
7	.4488	.2244	.1429	.2857	.1653	.3081
8	.3927	.1963	.1250	.2500	.1446	.2696
9	.3491	.1745	.1111	.2222	.1286	.2397
10	.3142	.1571	.1000	.2000	.1157	.2157
11	.2856	.1428	.0909	.1818	.1052	.1961
12	.2618	.1309	.0833	.1666	.0964	.1798
13	.2417	.1208	.0769	.1538	.0890	.1659
14	.2244	.1122	.0714	.1429	.0826	.1541

TABLE OF TOOTH PARTS—Continued.

DIAMETRAL PITCH IN FIRST COLUMN.

Diametral Pitch.	Circular Pitch.	Thickness of Tooth on Pitch Line.	Addendum $s = \frac{1}{P}$	Working Depth of Tooth.	Depth of Space below Pitch Line.	Whole Depth of Tooth.
P.	P'.	t.	s.	D".	s+f.	D"+f.
15	.2094	.1047	.0666	.1333	.0771	.1438
16	.1963	.0982	.0625	.1250	.0723	.1348
17	.1848	.0924	.05 8	.1176	.0681	.1269
18	.1745	.0873	.0555	.1111	.0643	.1198
19	.1653	.0827	.0526	.1053	.0609	.1135
20	.1571	.0785	.0500	.1000	.0579	.1079
22	.1428	.0714	.0455	.0909	.0526	.0980
24	.1309	.0654	.0417	.0833	.0482	.0898
26	.1208	.0604	.0385	.0769	.0445	.0829
28	.1122	.0561	.0357	.0714	.0413	.0770
30	.1047	.0524	.0333	.0666	.0386	.0719
32	.0982	.0491	.0312	.0625	.0362	.0674
34	.0924	.0462	.0294	.0588	.0340	.0634
36	.0873	.0436	.0278	.0555	.0321	.0599
38	.0827	.0413	.0263	.0526	.0304	.0568
40	.0785	.0393	.0250	.0500	.0289	.0539
42	.0748	.0374	.0238	.0476	.0275	.0514
44	.0714	.0357	.0227	.0455	.0263	.0490
46	.0683	.0341	.0217	.0435	.0252	.0469
48	.0654	.0327	.0208	.0417	.0241	.0449
50	.0628	.0314	.0200	.0400	.0231	.0431
56	.0561	.0280	.0178	.0357	.0207	.0385
60	.0524	.0262	.0166	.0333	.0193	.0360

PART II.

CHAPTER I.
TANGENT OF ARC AND ANGLE.

In PART II. we shall show how to calculate some of the functions of a right-angle triangle from a table of circular functions, the application of these calculations in some chapters of PART I. and in sizing blanks and cutting teeth of spiral gears, the selection of cutters for spiral gears, the application of continued fractions to some problems in gear wheels and cutting odd screw-threads, etc., etc. Subjects to be explained.

A Function is a quantity that depends upon another quantity for its value. Thus the amount a workman earns is a function of the time he has worked and of his wages per hour. Function defined.

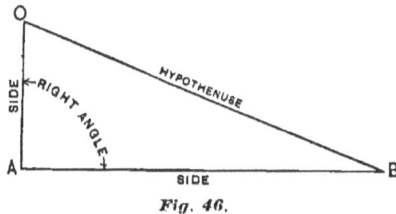

Fig. 46.

In any *right-angle triangle*, O A B, we shall, for convenience, call the two lines that form the right angle O A B the *sides*, instead of base and perpendicular. Thus O A B, being the right angle we call the line O A a side, and the line A B a side also. Right-angle Triangle.

When we speak of the angle A O B, we call the line O A the *side adjacent*. When we are speaking of the angle A B O we call the line A B the side adjacent. The line opposite the right angle is the *hypothenuse*. Side adjacent. Hypothenuse.

Tangent.

The Tangent of an arc is the line that touches it at one extremity and is terminated by a line drawn from the center through the other extremity. The tangent is always *outside* the arc and is also perpendicular to the radius which meets it at the point of tangency.

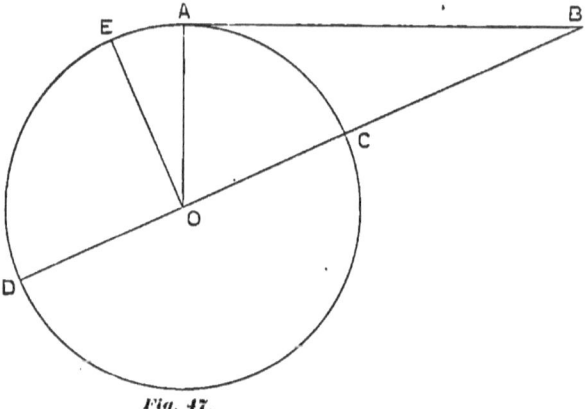

Fig. 47.

Thus, in Fig. 46, the line A B is the tangent of the arc A C. The point of tangency is at A.

An angle at the center of a circle is measured by the arc intercepted by the sides of the angle. Hence the tangent A B of the arc A C is also the tangent of the angle A O B.

In the tables of circular functions the radius of the arc is unity, or, in common practice, we take it as one inch. The radius O A being 1", if we know the length of the line or tangent A B we can, by looking in a table of tangents, find the number of degrees in the angle A O B.

To find the Degrees in an Angle. Thus, if A B is 2.25" long, we find the angle A O B is 66° very nearly. That is, having found that 2.2460 is the nearest number to 2.25 in the table of tangents at the end of this volume, we find the corresponding degrees of the angle in the column at the left hand of the table and the minutes to be added at the top of the column containing the 2.2460.

The table gives angles for every 10', which is sufficient for most purposes.

Now, if we have a right-angle triangle with an angle the same as O A B, but with O A two inches long, the line A B will also be twice as long as the tangent of angle A O B, as found in a table of tangents.

Let us take a triangle with the side O A = 5" long, and the side A B = 8" long; what is the number of degrees in the angle A O B? *Example to find the Degrees in an Angle.*

Dividing 8" by 5 we find what would be the length of A B if O A was only 1" long. The quotient then would be the length of tangent when the *radius* is 1" long, as in the table of tangents. 8 divided by 5 is 1.6. The nearest tangent in the table is 1.6003 and the corresponding angle is 58°, which would be the angle A O B when A B is 8" and the radius O A is 5" very nearly. The difference in the angles for tangents 1.6003 and 1.6 could hardly be seen in practice. The side opposite the required acute angle corresponds to the tangent and the side adjacent corresponds to the radius. Hence the rule:

To find the tangent of either acute angle in a right-angle triangle: *Divide the side opposite the angle by the side adjacent the angle and the quotient will be the tangent of the angle.* This rule should be committed to memory. Having found the tangent of the angle, the angle can be taken from the table of tangents. *To find the Tangent.*

The complement of an angle is the remainder after subtracting the angle from 90°. Thus 40° is the complement of 50°. *Complement of an Angle.*

The Cotangent of an angle is the tangent of the complement of the angle. Thus, in Fig. 47, the line A B is the cotangent of A O E. In right-angle triangles either acute angle is the complement of the other acute angle. Hence, if we know one acute angle, by subtracting this angle from 90° we get the other acute angle. As the arc approaches 90° the tangent becomes longer, and at 90° it is infinitely long. *Cotangent.*

The sign of infinity is ∞. Tangent 90° = ∞.

<small>To lay out an Angle by the Tangent. Example, Fig. 49.</small>
By a table of tangents, angles can be laid out upon sheet zinc, etc. This is often an advantage, as it is not convenient to lay protractor flat down so as to mark angles up to a sharp point. If we could lay off the length of a line *exactly* we could take tangents direct from table and obtain angle at once. It, however, is generally better to multiply the tangent by 5 or 10 and make an enlarged triangle. If, then, there is a slight error in laying off length of lines it will not make so much difference with the angle.

Let it be required to lay off an angle of 14° 30′. By the table we find the tangent to be .25861. Multiplying .25861 by 5 we obtain, in the enlarged triangle, 1.29305″ as the length of side opposite the angle 14° 30′. As we have made the side opposite five times as large, we must make the side *adjacent* five times as large, in order to keep angle the same. Hence, Fig. 48, draw the line A B 5″ long; perpendicular to this line at A draw the line A O 1.293″ long; now draw the line O B, and the angle A B O will be 14° 30′.

If special accuracy is required, the tangent can be multiplied by 10; the line A O will then be 2.586″ long and the line A B 10″ long. Remembering that the acute angles of a right-angle triangle are the complements of each other, we subtract 14° 30′ from 90′ and obtain 75° 30′ as the angle of A O B.

The reader will remember these angles as occurring in Part I., Chapter IV., and obtained in a different way. A semicircle upon the line O B touching the extremities O and B will just touch the right angle at A, and the line O B is four times as long as O A.

Let it be required to turn a piece 4″ long, 1″ diameter at small end, with a taper of 10° one side with the other; what will be the diameter of the piece at the large end?

<small>To calculate Diameter of a Tapering piece. Fig. 50.</small>
A section, Fig. 49, through the axis of this piece is the same as if we added two right-angle triangles, O A B and O′ A′ B′, to a straight piece A′ A B B′, 1″ wide and 4″ long, the acute angles B and B′ being 5°, thus making the sides O B and O′ B′ 10° with each other.

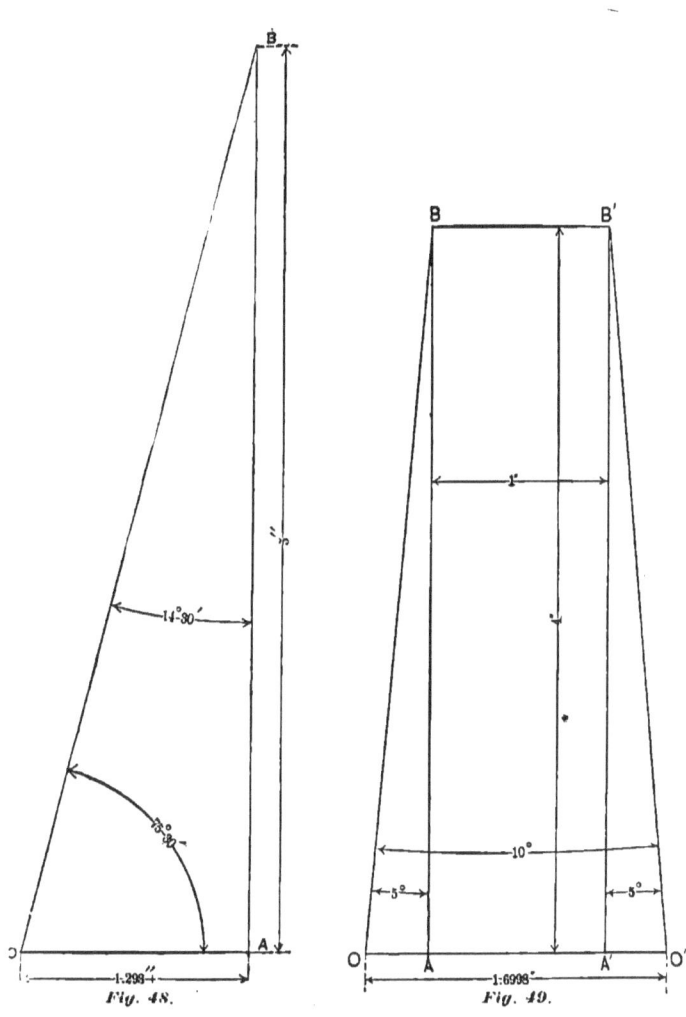

Fig. 48.   Fig. 49.

The tangent of 5° is .08748, which, multiplied by 4", gives .34992" as the length of each line, A O and A' O', to be added to 1" at the large end. Taking twice .34992" and adding to 1" we obtain 1.69984" as the diameter of large end.

This chapter must be thoroughly studied before taking up the next chapters. If once the memory becomes confused as to the tangent and sine of an angle, it will take much longer to get righted than it will to first carefully learn to recognize the tangent of an angle at *once*.

If one knows what the tangent *is*, he can better tell the functions that are *not* tangents.

CHAPTER II.

SINE—COSINE AND SECANT: SOME OF THEIR APPLICATIONS IN MACHINE CONSTRUCTION.

The Sine of an arc is the line drawn from one extremity of the arc to the diameter passing through the other extremity, the line being perpendicular to the diameter.

Another definition is: The sine of an arc is the distance of one extremity of the arc from the diameter, through the other extremity.

The sine of an angle is the sine of the arc that measures the angle. <small>Sine of Arc and Angle.</small>

In Fig. 50, A C is the sine of the arc B C, and of the angle B O C. It will be seen that the sine is always inside of the arc, and can never be longer than the radius. As the arc approaches 90°, the sine comes nearer to the radius, and at 90° the sine is equal to 1, or is the radius itself. From the definition of a sine, the *side* A C, opposite the angle A O C, in *any* right-angle triangle, is the sine of the angle A O C, when O C is the *radius* of the arc.

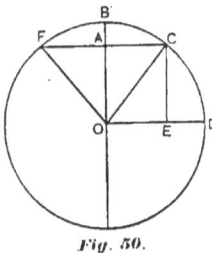

Fig. 50.

Hence the rule: *In any right-angle triangle, the side opposite either acute angle, divided by the hypothenuse, is equal to the sine of the angle.* <small>To find the Sine.</small>

The quotient thus obtained is the length of side opposite the angle when the hypothenuse or radius is unity. The rule should be carefully committed to memory.

Chord of an Arc. *A Chord* is a straight line joining the extremities of an arc, and is twice as long as the sine of half the angle measured by the arc. Thus, in Fig. 51, the chord F C is twice as long as the sine A C.

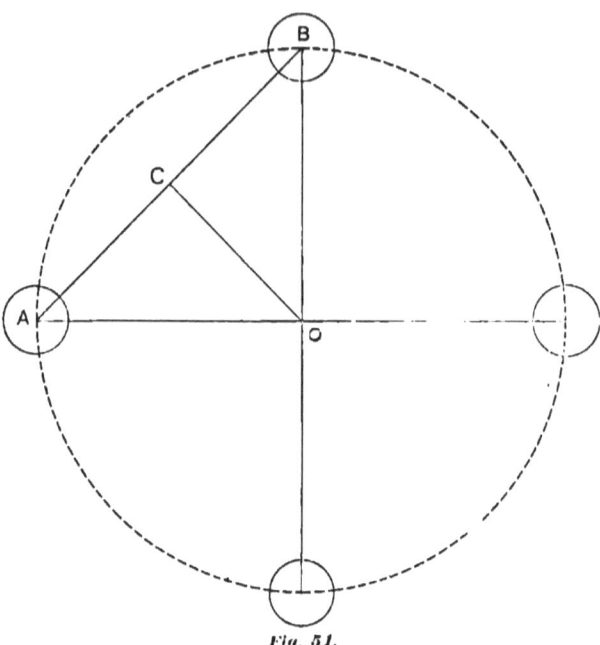

Fig. 51.

Let there be four holes equidistant about a circle 3" in diameter—Fig. 51; what is the shortest distance between two holes? This shortest distance is the **Example to find the Chord.** chord A B, which is twice the sine of the angle C O B. The angle A O B is one-quarter of the circle, and C O B is one-eighth of the circle. 360°, divided by 8=45°, the angle C O B. The sine of 45° is .70710, which multiplied by the radius 1.5", gives length C B in the circle, 3" in diameter, as 1.06065". Twice this length is the required distance A B=2.1213".

When a cylindrical piece is to be cut into any number of sides, the foregoing operation can be applied to obtain the width of one side. A plane figure bounded **Polygon.** by straight lines is called a polygon.

When the outside diameter and the number of sides of a regular polygon are given, to find the length of one of the sides: *Divide 360° by twice the number of sides ; multiply the sine of the quotient by the outer diameter, and the product will be the length of one of the sides.* To find the length of Side.

Multiplying by the diameter is the same as multiplying by the radius, and that product again by 2.

The Cosine of an angle is the sine of the complement of the angle. Cosine.

In Fig. 50, C O D is the complement of the angle A O C; the line C E is the sine of C O D, and hence is the cosine of B O C. The line O A is equal to C E. It is quite as well to remember the cosine as the part of the radius, from the center that is cut off by the sine. Thus the sine A C of the angle A O C cuts off the cosine O A. The line O A may be called the cosine because it is equal to the cosine C E.

In any right-angle triangle, the side adjacent either acute angle corresponds to the cosine when the hypothenuse is the radius of the arc that measures the angle; hence: *Divide the side adjacent the acute angle by the hypothenuse, and the quotient will be the cosine of the angle.* To find the Cosine.

When a cylindrical piece is cut into a polygon of any number of sides, a table of cosines can be used to get the diameter across the sides. Length of sides of Polygon.

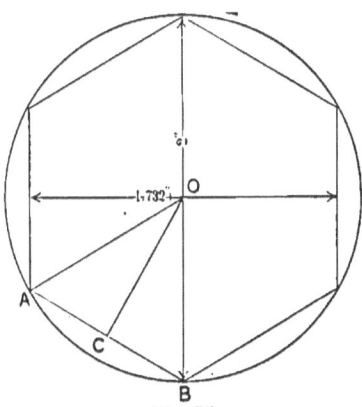

Fig. 52.

Let a cylinder, 2" diameter, Fig. 53, be cut six-sided; what is the diameter across the sides?

The angle A O B, at the center, occupied by one of these sides, is one-sixth of the circle, =60°. The cosine of one-half this angle, 30°, is the line C O; twice this line is the diameter across the sides. The cosine of 30° is .86602, which, multiplied by 2, gives 1.73204" as the diameter across the sides.

Of course, if the radius is other than unity, the cosine should be multiplied by the radius, and the product again by 2, in order to get diameter across the sides; or what is the same thing, multiply the cosine by the whole diameter or the diameter across the corners.

Rule for Diameter across sides of a Polygon. The rule for obtaining the diameter across sides of regular polygon, when the diameter across corners is given, will then be: *Multiply the cosine of 360° divided by twice the number of sides, by the diameter across corners, and the product will be the diameter across sides.*

Look at the right-hand column for degrees of the cosine, and at bottom of page for minutes to add to the degrees.

Secant. *The Secant* of an arc is a straight line drawn from the center through one end of an arc, and terminated by a tangent drawn from the other end of the arc.

Thus, in Fig. 53, the line O B is the secant of the angle C O B.

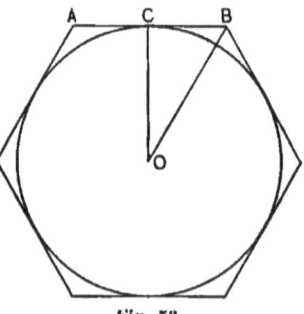

Fig. 53.

To find the Secant. In any right-angle triangle, *divide the hypothenuse by the side adjacent either acute angle, and the quotient will be the secant of that angle.*

That is, if we divide the distance O B by O C, in the right-angle triangle C O B, the quotient will be the secant of the angle C O B.

The secant cannot be less than the radius; it increases as the angle increases, and at 90° the secant is infinity=∞.

A six-sided piece is to be 1½″ across the sides; how large must a blank be turned before cutting the sides? Dividing 360° by twice the number of sides, we have 30°, which is the angle C O B. The secant of 30° is 1.1547.

To find the Diameter across corners of a Polygon.

The radius of the six-sided piece is .75″.

Multiplying the secant 1.1547 by .75″, we obtain the length of radius of the blank O B; multiplying again by 2, we obtain the diameter 1.732″+.

Hence, in a regular polygon, when the diameter across sides and the number of sides are given, to find diameter across corners: *Multiply the secant of 360° divided by twice the number of sides, by the diameter across sides, and the product will be the diameter across corners.*

It will be seen that the side taken as a divisor has been in each case the side corresponding to the radius of the arc that subtends the angle.

The *versed sine* of an acute angle is the part of radius outside the sine, or it is the radius *minus* the cosine. Thus, in Fig. 50, the versed sine of the arc BC is AB. The versed sine is not given in the tables of circular functions: when it is wanted for any angle less than 90° we subtract the cosine of that angle from the radius 1. Having it for the radius 1, we can multiply by the radius of any other arc of which we may wish to know the versed sine.

Fig. 54 is a sketch of a gear tooth of 1P. In measuring gear teeth of coarse pitch it is sometimes a convenience to know the chordal thickness of the tooth, as at ATB, because it may be enough shorter than the regular tooth-thickness AHB, or t, to require attention. It may be also well to know the versed sine of the angle B, or the distance H, in order to tell where to measure the chordal thickness.

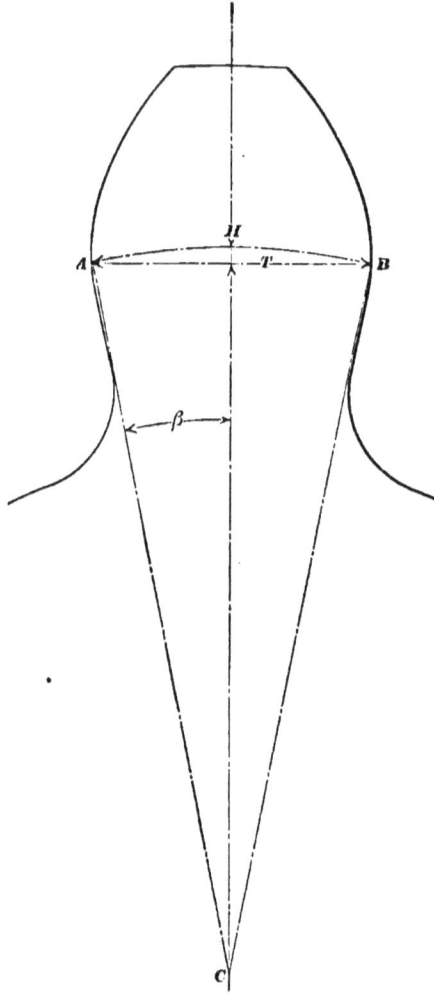

Fig. 54.

On pages 104 and 105 are tables of data pertaining to chordal thickness of 1P. teeth. For any other diametral pitch, divide the number in the table by that pitch.

CHORDAL THICKNESS OF TEETH FOR GEARS AND CUTTERS,
ON A BASIS OF 1 DIAMETRAL PITCH.

N = Number of teeth in gears.
T = Chordal thickness of Tooth. $T = D \sin \beta'$
H = Height of Arc. $H = R (1 - \cos \beta')$.
D = Pitch Diameter.
R = Pitch Radius.
β' = 90° divided by the number of teeth.

NOTE.—When the tooth of a gear is measured, add the height of arc to (S); and when gear cutter is measured subtract the height of arc from (S + f).

INVOLUTE.

Cutter.	T	H	Corrected S+f for Cutt.	Corrected S for Gear.
No. 1 —135 T — 1 P	1.5707	.0047	1.1524	1.0047
" 2 — 55 T — 1 P	1.5706	.0112	1.1459	1.0112
" 3 — 35 T — 1 P	1.5702	.0176	1.1395	1.0176
" 4 — 26 T — 1 P	1.5698	.0237	1.1334	1.0237
" 5 — 21 T — 1 P	1.5694	.0294	1.1277	1.0294
" 6 — 17 T — 1 P	1.5686	.0362	1.1209	1.0362
" 7 — 14 T — 1 P	1.5675	.0440	1.1131	1.0440
" 8 — 12 T — 1 P	1.5663	.0514	1.1057	1.0514
11 T — 1 P	1.5654	.0559	1.1011	1.0559
10 T — 1 P	1.5643	.0616	1.0955	1.0616
9 T — 1 P	1.5628	.0684	1.0887	1.0684
8 T — 1 P	1.5607	.0769	1.0802	1.0769

EPICYCLOIDAL.

Cutter.	T	H	Corrected S + f for Cutt.	Corrected S for Gear.
A —	12 T — 1 P	1.5663	.0514	1.1057	1.0514
B —	13 T — 1 P	1.5670	.0474	1.1097	1.0474
C —	14 T — 1 P	1.5675	.0440	1.1131	1.0440
D —	15 T — 1 P	1.5679	.0411	1.1160	1.0411
E —	16 T — 1 P	1.5683	.0385	1.1186	1.0385
F —	17 T — 1 P	1.5686	.0362	1.1209	1.0362
G —	18 T — 1 P	1.5688	.0342	1.1229	1.0342
H —	19 T — 1 P	1.5690	.0324	1.1247	1.0324
I —	20 T — 1 P	1.5692	.0308	1.1263	1.0308
J —	21 T — 1 P	1.5694	.0294	1.1277	1.0294
K —	23 T — 1 P	1.5696	.0268	1.1303	1.0268
L —	25 T — 1 P	1.5698	.0247	1.1324	1.0247
M —	27 T — 1 P	1.5699	.0228	1.1343	1.0228
N —	30 T — 1 P	1.5701	.0208	1.1363	1.0208
O —	34 T — 1 P	1.5703	.0181	1.1390	1.0181
P —	38 T — 1 P	1.5703	.0162	1.1409	1.0162
Q —	43 T — 1 P	1.5705	.0143	1.1428	1.0143
R —	50 T — 1 P	1.5705	.0123	1.1448	1.0123
S —	60 T — 1 P	1.5706	.0102	1.1469	1.0102
T —	75 T — 1 P	1.5707	.0083	1.1488	1.0083
U —	100 T — 1 P	1.5707	.0060	1.1511	1.0060
V —	150 T — 1 P	1.5707	.0045	1.1526	1.0045
W —	250 T — 1 P	1.5708	.0025	1.1546	1.0025

SPECIAL.

No. Teeth.	T	H	Corrected S + f for Cutt.	Corrected S for Gear.
9 T — 1 P	1.5628	.0684	1.0887	1.0684
10 T — 1 P	1.5643	.0616	1.0955	1.0616
11 T — 1 P	1.5654	.0559	1.1012	1.0559

CHAPTER III.

APPLICATION OF CIRCULAR FUNCTIONS—WHOLE DIAMETER OF BEVEL GEAR BLANKS—ANGLES OF BEVEL GEAR BLANKS.

The rules given in this chapter apply only to bevel gears having the center angle $c'\,O\,i$ not greater than 90°. To avoid confusion we will illustrate one gear only. The same rules apply to all sizes of bevel gears. Fig. 55 is the outline of a pinion 4 P, 20 teeth, to mesh with a gear 28 teeth, shafts at right angles. For making sketch of bevel gears see Chapter IX., Part I.

In Fig. 55, the line O $m'\,m$ is continued to the line $a\,b$. The angle $c'\,O\,i$ that the cone pitch-line makes with the center line may be called the *center angle*.

Angle of Edge. Fig. 55. The center angle $c'\,O\,i$ is equal to the angle of edge $c'\,i\,c$. $c'\,i$ is the side opposite the center angle $c'\,O\,i$, and $c'\,O$ is the side adjacent the center angle. $c'\,i = 2.5''$; $c'\,O = 3.5''$. Dividing 2.5" by 3.5" we obtain .71428" + as the tangent of $c'\,O\,i$. In the table we find .71329 to be the nearest tangent, the corresponding angle being 35° 30'. 35½°, then, is the center angle $c'\,O\,i$ and the angle of edge $c'\,i\,n$, very nearly.

When the axes of bevel gears are at right angles the angle of edge of one gear is the complement of angle of edge of the other gear. Subtracting, then, 35½° from 90° we obtain 54½° as the angle of edge of gear 28 teeth, to mesh with gear 20 teeth, Fig. 55, from which we have the rule for obtaining centre angles when the axes of gears are at right angles.

Divide the radius of the pinion by the radius of the gear and the quotient will be the tangent of centre angle of the pinion.

Now subtract this centre angle from 90 deg. and we have the centre angle of the gear.

The same result is obtained by dividing the number of teeth in the pinion by the number of teeth in the gear; the quotient is the tangent of the centre angle.

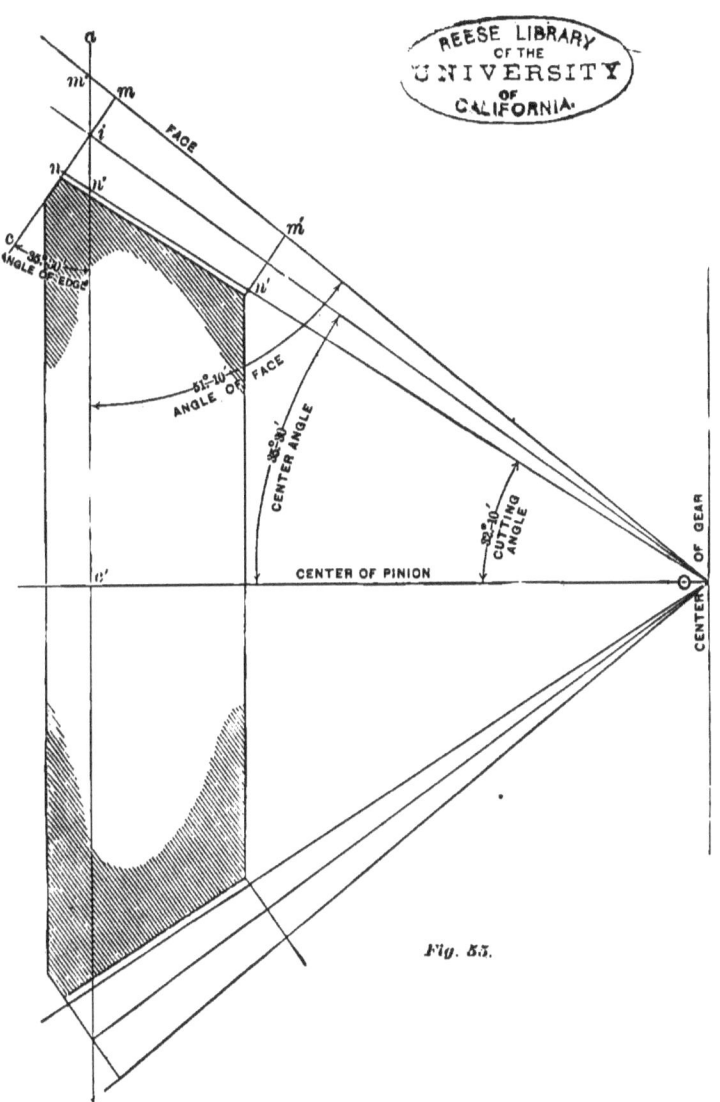

Fig. 55.

Angle of Face. To obtain angle of face $O\,m''\,c'$, the distance $c'\,O$ becomes the side opposite and the distance $m''\,c'$ is the side adjacent.

The distance $c'\,O$ is $3.5''$, the radius of the 28 tooth bevel gear. The distance $c'\,m''$ is by measurement $2.82''$.

Dividing 3.5 by 2.82 we obtain 1.2411 for tangent of angle of face $O\,m''\,c'$. The nearest tangent in the table is 1.2422 and the corresponding angle is $51°\,10'$. To obtain cutting angle $c'\,O\,n''$ we divide the distance $c'\,n''$ by $c'\,O$. By measurement $c'\,n''$ is $2.2''$. Dividing 2.2 by 3.5 we obtain .62857 for tangent of cutting angle. The nearest corresponding angle in the table is $32°10'$.

The largest pitch diameter, kj, of a bevel gear, as in Fig. 56, is known the same as the pitch diameter of any spur gear. Now, if we know the distance $b\,o$ or its equal $a\,q$, we can obtain the whole diameter of bevel gear blank by adding twice the distance $b\,o$ to the largest pitch diameter.

Diameter Increment. Fig. 56. Twice the distance $b\,o$, or what is the same thing, the sum of $a\,q$ and $b\,o$ is called the *diameter increment*, because it is the amount by which we increase the largest pitch diameter to obtain the whole or outside diameter of bevel gear blanks. The distance $b\,o$ can be calculated without measuring the diagram.

The angle $b\,o\,j$ is equal to the angle of edge.

The angle of edge, it will be remembered, is the angle formed by outer edge of blank or ends of teeth with the end of hub or a plane perpendicular to the axis of gear.

The distance $b\,o$ is equal to the cosine of angle of edge, multiplied by the distance $j\,o$. The distance $j\,o$ is the addendum, as in previous chapters ($=s$).

Hence the rule for obtaining the diameter increment of any bevel gear: *Multiply the cosine of angle of edge by the working depth of teeth* (D'), *and the product will be the diameter increment.*

By the method given in Chapter II. we find the angle of edge of gear (Fig. 56) is $56°\,20'$. The cosine of $56°\,20'$ is .55436, which, multiplied by $\frac{3}{4}''$, or the **Outside Diameter.** depth of the 3 P gear, gives the diameter increment of the bevel gear 18 teeth, 3 P meshing with pinion of 12

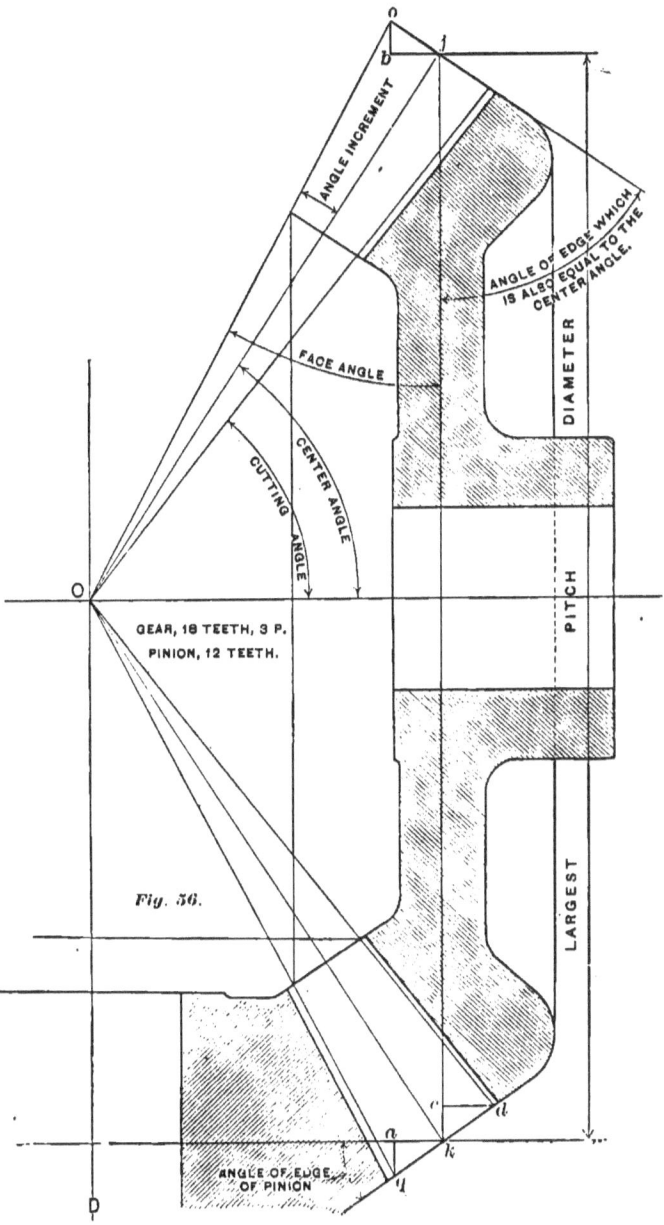

Fig. 56.

GEAR, 18 TEETH, 3 P.
PINION, 12 TEETH.

teeth. ⅔ of .55436=.369″+ (or .37″, nearly). Adding the diameter increment, .37″, to the largest pitch diameter of gear, 6″, we have 6.37″ as the outside diameter.

In the same manner, the distance $c\,d$ is half the diameter increment of the pinion. The angle $c\,d\,k$ is equal to the center angle of pinion, and when axes are at right angles is the complement of center angle of gear. The center angle of pinion is 33° 40′. The cosine, multiplied by the working depth, gives .555″ for diameter increment of pinion, and we have 4.555″ for outside diameter of pinion.

In turning bevel gear blanks, it is sufficiently accurate to make the diameter to the nearest hundredth of an inch.

Angle Increment. The small angle $o\,O\,j$ is called the *angle increment*. When shafts are at right angles the face angle of one gear is equal to the center angle of the other gear, *minus* the angle increment.

Thus the angle of face of gear (Fig. 56) is less than the center angle $D\,O\,k$, or its equal $O\,j\,k$ by the angle $o\,O\,j$. That is, subtracting $o\,O\,j$ from $O\,j\,k$, the remainder will be the angle of face of gear.

Subtracting the angle increment from the center angle of gear, the remainder will be the cutting angle.

The angle increment can be obtained by dividing $o\,j$, the side opposite, by $O\,j$, the side adjacent, thus finding the tangent as usual.

The length of cone-pitch line from the common center, O to j, can be found, without measuring diagram, by multiplying the secant of angle $O\,j\,k$, or the center angle of pinion, by the radius of largest pitch diameter of gear.

The secant of angle $O\,j\,k$, 33° 40′, is 1.2015, which, multiplied by 3″, the radius of gear, gives 3.6045″ as the length of line $O\,j$.

Dividing $o\,j$ by $O\,j$, we have for tangent .0924, and for angle increment 5° 20′.

The angle increment can also be obtained by the following rule:

Divide the sine of center angle by half the number of teeth, and the quotient will be the tangent of increment angle.

Subtracting the angle increment from center angles of gear and pinion, we have respectively:

Cutting angle of gear, 51°.
Cutting angle of pinion, 28° 20'.

Remembering that when the shafts are at right angles, the face angle of a gear is equal to the cutting angle of its mate (Chapter X. part 1), we have:

Face angle of gear, 28° 20'.
Face angle of pinion, 51°.

It will be seen that both the whole diameter and the angles of bevel gears can be obtained without making a diagram. Mr. George B. Grant has made a table of different pairs of gears from 1 to 1 up to 10 to 1, containing diameter increments, angle increments and center angles, and has published it in the *American Machinist* of October 31, 1885. We have adopted the terms "diameter increment," "angle increment" and "center angle" from him. He uses the term "*back angle*" for what we have called *angle of edge*, only he measures the angle from the axis of the gear, instead of from the side of the gear or from the end of hub, as we have done; that is, his "back angle" is the complement of our *angle of edge*.

To lay out an Angle by the Sine.

In laying out angles, the following method may be preferred, as it does away with the necessity of making a right angle: Draw a circle, A B O (Fig. 57), ten

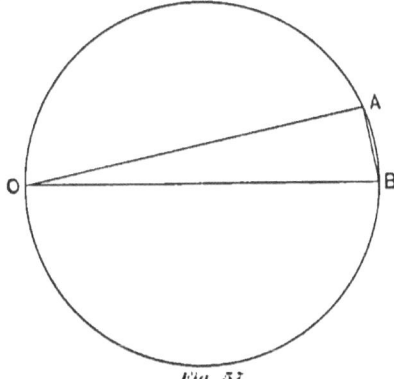

Fig. 57.

inches in diameter. Set the dividers to ten times the sine of the required angle, and point off this distance in the circumference as at A B. From any point O in the circumference, draw the lines O A and O B. The angle A O B is the angle required. Thus, let the required angle be 12°. The sine of 12° is .20791, which, multiplied by 10, gives 2.0791", or $2\frac{8}{100}$" nearly, for the distance A B.

Any diameter of circle can be taken if we multiply the sine by the diameter, but 10" is very convenient, as all we have to do with the sine is to move the decimal point one place to the right.

If either of the lines pass through the centre, then the two lines which do not pass through the centre will form a right angle. Thus, if O B passes through the centre then the two lines A B and A O will form a right angle at A.

CHAPTER IV.

SPIRAL GEARS—CALCULATIONS FOR PITCH OF SPIRALS.

When the teeth of a gear are cut, not in a straight *Spiral Gear.* path, like a spur gear, but in a helical or screw-like path, the gear is called, technically, a twisted or screw gear, but more generally among mechanics, a spiral gear. A distinction is sometimes made between a screw gear and a twisted gear. In twisted gears the pitch surfaces roll upon each other, exactly like spur gears, the axes being parallel, the same as in Fig. 1, Part I. In screw gears there is an end movement, or slipping of the pitch surfaces upon each other, the axes not being parallel. In screw gearing the action is analogous to a screw and nut, one gear driving another by the end movement of its tooth path. This is readily seen in the case of a worm and worm-wheel, when the axes are at right angles, as the movement of wheel is then wholly due to the end movement of worm thread. But, as we make the axes of gears more nearly parallel, they may still be screw gears, but the distinction is not so readily seen.

We can have two gears that are alike run together, with their axes at right angles, as at A B, Fig. 59.

The same gear may be used in a train of screw gears or in a train of twisted gears. Thus, B, as it relates to A, may be called a screw gear; but in connection with C, the same gear, B, may be called a twisted gear. These distinctions are not usually made, and we call all helical or screw-like gears made on the Universal Milling Machine *spiral gears*.

When two external spiral gears run together, with *Direction of Spiral with reference to Axes.* their axes parallel, the teeth of the gears must have opposite hand spirals. *Fig. 59.*

Thus, in Fig. 59 the gear B has right hand spiral teeth, and the gear C has left hand spiral teeth. When the axes of two spiral gears are at right angles, both gears must have the same hand spiral teeth. A and B, Fig. 59, have right hand spiral teeth. If both gears A and B had left hand spiral teeth, the relative direction in which they turn would be reversed.

Spiral Pitch. The spiral pitch or pitch of spiral is the distance the spiral advances in one turn. Strictly, this is the *lead* of the spiral. A cylinder or gear cut with spiral grooves is merely a screw of coarse pitch or long lead; that is, a spiral is a coarse pitch screw, and a screw is a fine pitch spiral.

Since the introduction and extensive use of the Universal Milling Machine, it has become customary to call any screw cut in the milling machine a spiral. The spiral pitch is given as so many inches to one turn. Thus, a cylinder having a spiral groove that advances six inches to one turn, is said to have a six inch spiral.

In screws the pitch is often given as so many threads to one inch. Thus, a screw of $\frac{1}{2}''$ lead is said to be 2 threads to the inch. The reciprocal expression is not much used with spirals. For example, it would not be convenient to speak of a spiral of 6" lead, as $\frac{1}{6}$ threads to one inch.

The calculations for spirals are made from the functions of a right angle triangle.

Example, showing the nature of a Helix or Spiral. Cut from paper a right angle triangle, one side of the right angle 6" long, and the other side of the right angle 2". Make a cylinder 6" in circumference. It will be remembered (Part I., Chapter II.) that the circumference of a cylinder, multiplied by .3183, equals the diameter—$6'' \times .3183 = 1.9098''$. Wrap the paper triangle around the cylinder, letting the 2" side be parallel to the axis, the 6" side perpendicular to the axis and reaching around the cylinder. The hypotheneuse now forms a helix or screw-like line, called a spiral. Fasten the paper triangle thus wrapped around. See Fig. 60.

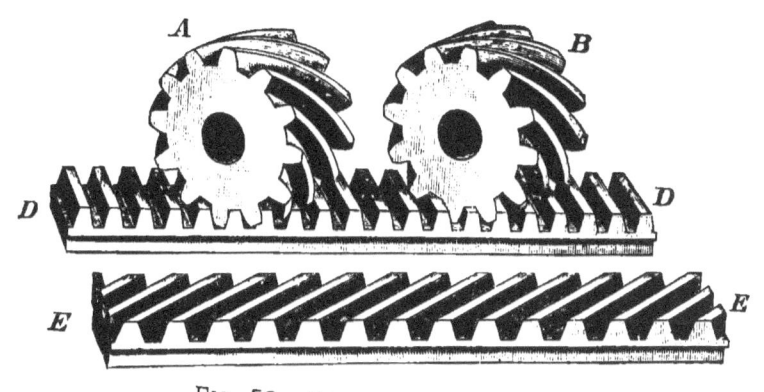

FIG. 58.—RACKS AND GEARS.

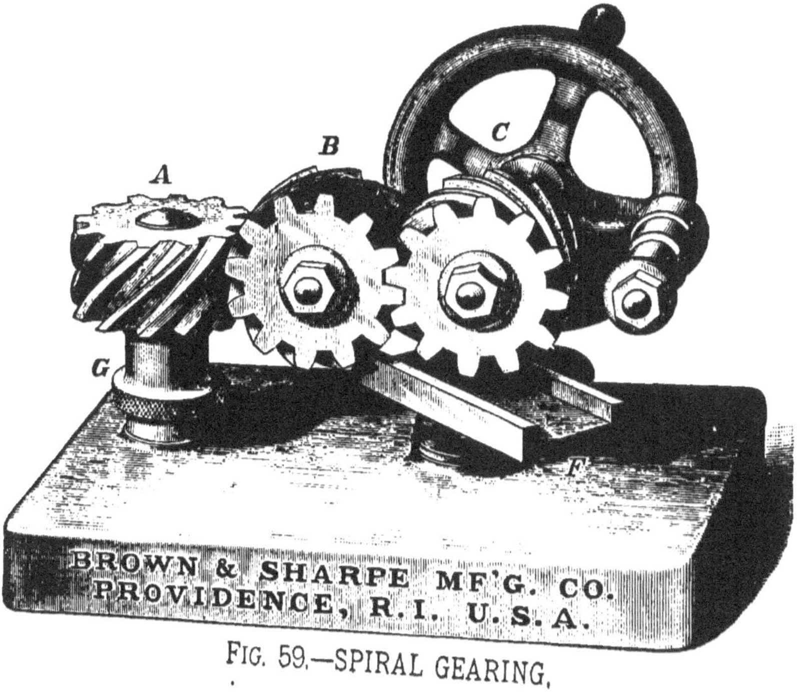

FIG. 59.—SPIRAL GEARING.

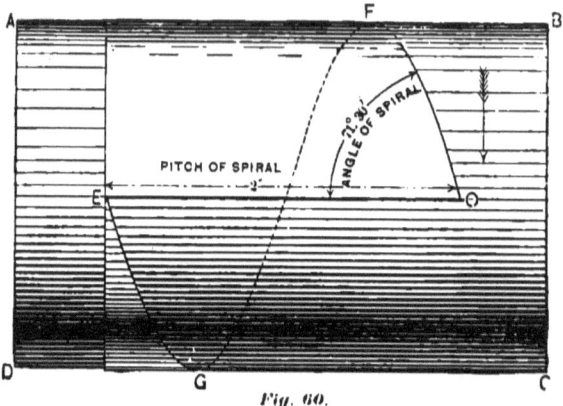

Fig. 60.

If we now turn this cylinder A B C D in the direction of the arrow, the spiral will advance from O to E. This advance is the *pitch of the spiral*.

The angle E O F, which the spiral makes with the axis E O, is the *angle of the spiral*. This angle is found as in Chapter I. The circumference of the cylinder corresponds to the side *opposite the angle*. The pitch of the spiral corresponds to the side *adjacent the angle*. Hence the rule for getting angle of spiral:

Rules for calculating the parts of a Spiral. *Divide the circumference of the cylinder or spiral by the number of inches of spiral to one turn, and the quotient will be the tangent of angle of spiral.*

When the angle of spiral and circumference are given, to find the pitch:

Divide the circumference by the tangent of angle, and the quotient will be the pitch of the spiral.

When the angle of spiral and the lead or pitch of spiral are given, to find the circumference:

Multiply the tangent of angle by the pitch, and the product will be the circumference.

When applying calculations to spiral gears the angle is reckoned at the pitch circumference and not at the outer or addendum circle.

It will be seen that when two spirals of different diameters have the same pitch the spiral of less diameter will have the smaller angle. Thus in Fig. 60 if the paper triangle had been 4" long instead of 6" the diameter of the cylinder would have been 1.27" and the angle of the spiral would have been only 32½ degrees.

CHAPTER V.

EXAMPLES IN CALCULATION OF PITCH OF SPIRAL—ANGLE OF SPIRAL—CIRCUMFERENCE OF SPIRAL GEARS— A FEW HINTS ON CUTTING.

It will be seen that the rules for calculating circumference of spiral gears, angle and pitch of spiral are the same as in Chapter I, for tangent and angle of a right angle triangle. In Chapter IV the word "circumference" is substituted for "side opposite," and the words "pitch of spiral" are substituted for side "adjacent."

When two spiral gears are in mesh the angle of spiral should be the same in one gear as in the other, in order to have the shafts parallel and the teeth work properly together. When two gears both have right hand spiral teeth, or both have left hand spiral teeth, the angle of their shafts will be equal to the *sum* of the angles of their spirals. But when two gears have different hand spirals the angle of their shafts will be equal to the *difference* of their angles of spirals. Thus, in Fig. 59 the gears A and B both have right hand spirals. The angle of both spirals is 45°, their sum is 90°, or their axes are at right angles. But C has a left hand spiral of 45°. Hence, as the difference between angles of spirals of B and C is 0, their axes are parallel. *Angles of Spirals with reference to Angle of Shafts.*

When the two gears have the same number of teeth the pitch of the spiral will be alike in both gears. But when one gear has more teeth than the other the pitch of spiral in the larger gear should be longer in the same ratio. Thus, if one gear has 50 teeth and the other gear has 25 teeth, the pitch of spiral in the 50 tooth wheel should be twice as long as that of the 25 *Pitch in Spirals of different Diameters.*

tooth wheel. Of course, the diameter of pitch circle should be twice as large in the 50 tooth as in the 25 tooth wheel.

In spirals where the angle is 45° the circumference is the same as the spiral pitch, because the tangent of 45° is 1.

Variation in Circumference to suit a Spiral. Sometimes the circumference is varied to suit a pitch that can be cut on the machine and retain the angle required. This would apply to cutting rolls for making diamond-shaped impressions where the diameter of the roll is not a matter of importance.

When two gears are to run together in a given velocity ratio, it is well to first select spirals that the machine will cut of the same ratio, and calculate the numbers of teeth and angle to correspond. This will often save considerable time in figuring.

The calculations for spiral gears present no special difficulties, but sometimes a little ingenuity is required to make work conform to the machine and to such cutters as we may have in stock. It is a good plan to make a trial piece for each gear, and to cut a few teeth in each trial piece to test the setting of the machine.

Dummies or Trial Pieces. These trial pieces are called "dummies." If the gears are likely to be duplicated, each dummy can be marked and kept for future setting of the machine. Stamp all the data on the dummies; it is better to spend a little time in marking dummies than a good deal of time hunting up, or trying to *remember*, old data.

Let it be required to make two spiral gears to run with a ratio of 4 to 1, the distance between centers to be $3.125''$ ($3\frac{1}{8}''$).

By rule given in Chapter XII., Part I., we find the diameters of pitch circles will be $5''$ and $1\frac{1}{4}''$. Let us take a spiral of $48''$ pitch for the large gear, and a spiral of $12''$ pitch for the small gear. The circumference of the $5''$ pitch circle is $15.70796''$. Dividing the circumference by the pitch of the spiral, we have $\frac{15.70796}{48} = .32724''$ for tangent of angle of spiral. In the table the nearest angle to tangent, $.32724''$, is $18°\ 10'$. As before stated, the angle of the teeth in the small gear will be the same as the angle of teeth or spiral in the large gear. Now, this rule gives the angle at the pitch surface only. Upon looking at a small screw of coarse pitch, it will be seen that the angle at bottom of the thread is not so great as the angle at top of thread; that is, the thread at bottom is nearer parallel to the center line than that at the top.

A difference in Angles at top and bottom of Spiral Grooves.

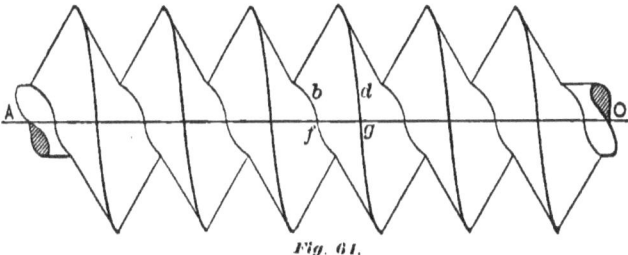

Fig. 61.

This will be seen in Fig. 61, where A O is the center line; $b\,f$ shows direction of bottom of the thread, and $d\,g$ shows direction of top of thread. The angle $A\,f\,b$ is less than the angle $A\,g\,d$. This difference of angle is due to the warped nature of a screw thread, and sometimes makes it necessary to change the angle for setting work from the figured angle, when a rotary disk cutter is used, to prevent the cutter from marring the groove as the teeth of cutter enter and leave. How much to change the angle can be seen by inspection when cutting the dummies. The change of angle will be more in a small gear of a given pitch than in a large gear of the same pitch.

A rotary disk cutter is generally preferable, because *Disk-cutters.* it cuts faster and holds its shape better. Yet it is hardly practical to cut low numbered pinions with rotary disk cutters, because for some distance below the pitch line the spaces are so nearly parallel. A part of the difficulty can be removed by making the cutter as small as is consistent with strength. Still more of the trouble can be done away with by making a cutter on a shank, the center of the work and the center of *Shank or End Cutter.* shank cutter then being in the same plane. When using a shank cutter the center of the work is perpendicular to the center of the cutter, no adjustment for angle being made. Strictly, a shank mill does not reproduce its own shape in cutting a spiral groove. In using a shank cutter, more care is necessary to see that the work does not slip. It may be well to rough out with a disk cutter and finish with a shank cutter. There is not generally much difficulty in involute or single-curve spiral gears with disk cutters.

Example in calculation of Pitch of Spiral. A cylinder $2''$ diameter is to have spiral grooves $20°$ with the center line of cylinder; what will be the pitch of spiral? The circumference is $6.2832''$. The tangent of $20°$ is $.36397$. Dividing the circumference by the tangent of angle, we obtain $\frac{6.2832}{.36397} = 17.26'' +$ for pitch of spiral.

Before cutting into a blank it is well to make a slight trace of the spiral, with the cutter, after the machine is geared up, to see if the gears are properly arranged. Attention to this may avoid spoiling a blank.

The cutting of spiral gears develops some curious facts to one who may not have studied warped surfaces.

In the Universal Milling Machine we can cut a class of warped surfaces that will fit a straight edge in two directions. Thus, in Fig. 61, if it were possible to reduce the diameter of screw and then cut the thread clear down to the center line A O, the bottom of the thread would be a straight line running through the center or the line A O itself. The sides would still be straight as in the figure. If we should cut a spiral groove with a plain rotary disk cutter, having parallel sides, the shape of the grooves would have but little resemblance to that of the cutter. Taking advantage of this principle, we learned the fact that spiral gears can be planed with a rack tool.

Spiral Gears cut with Rack Tool. The gears, Fig. 59, were planed. The tool was of the same shape as the spaces in the rack D D. All spiral gears of the same pitch could be planed with one tool.

The nature of this can be seen when we consider that straight rack teeth can mesh with spiral gears, as in Fig. 58.

We have succeeded in cutting small spiral gears with a long fly tool, cutting on one side only. The shape of this fly tool was like a common lathe side tool. In this case, of course, the gears had to be reversed in order to finish both sides of teeth. A description and an illustration of cutting spiral and spur gears with a fly tool on our Universal Milling Machine are in the *American Machinist* for Nov. 21, 1885.

CHAPTER VI.

NORMAL PITCH OF SPIRAL GEARS—CURVATURE OF PITCH SURFACE—FORM OF CUTTERS.

Normal to a Curve.   A Normal to a curve is a line perpendicular to the tangent at the point of tangency.

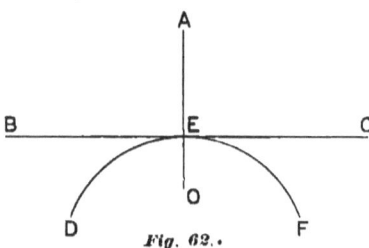

Fig. 62.

In Fig. 62, the line B C is tangent to the arc D E F, and the line A E O, being perpendicular to the tangent at E, the point of tangency, is a *normal* to the arc.

Fig. 63 is a representation of the pitch surface of a spiral gear. A' D' C' is the circular pitch, as in Part I. A D C is the same circular pitch seen upon the periphery of a wheel. Let A D be a tooth and D C a space. Now, to make this space D C, the path of cutting is along the dotted line *a b*. By mere inspection, we can see that the *shortest* distance between two teeth along the pitch surface is not the distance A D C.

Let the line A E B be perpendicular to the sides of teeth upon the pitch surface. A continuation of this line, perpendicular to all the teeth, is called the *Normal Helix*. The line A E B, reaching over a tooth and a space along the normal helix, is called the *Normal Pitch*.

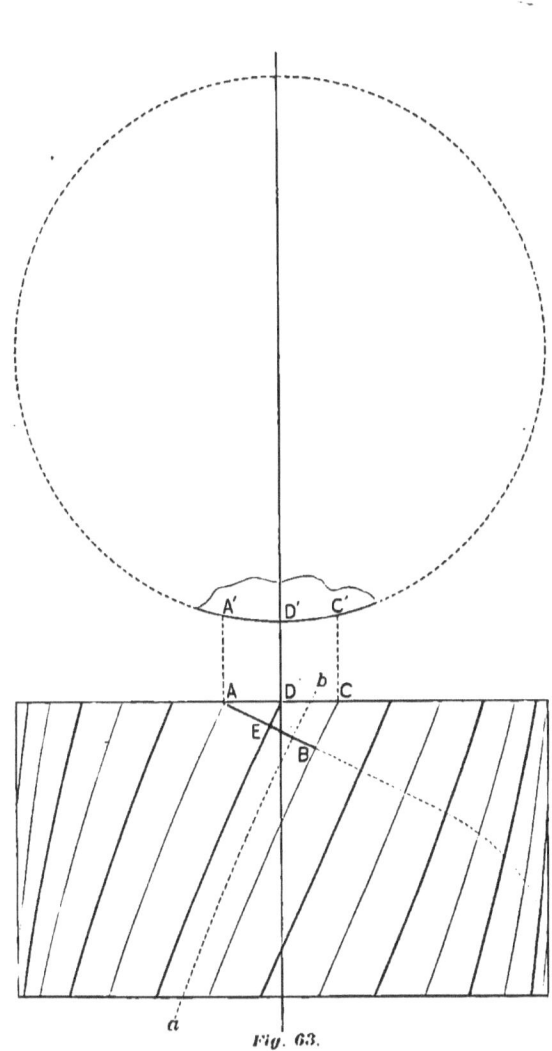

Fig. 63.

Normal Pitch. The *Normal Pitch* of a spiral gear is then: *The shortest distance between the centers of two consecutive teeth measured along the pitch surface.*

In spur gears the normal pitch and circular pitch are alike. In the rack D D, Fig. 58, the linear pitch and normal pitch are alike.

Cutter for Spiral Gears. From the foregoing it will be seen that, if we should cut the space D C with a cutter, the thickness of which at the pitch line is equal to one-half the *circular* pitch, as in spur wheels, the space would be too wide, and the teeth would be too thin. Hence, spiral gears should be cut with thinner cutters than spur gears of the same circular pitch.

The angle C A B is equal to the angle of the spiral. The line A E B corresponds to the *cosine* of the angle C A B. Hence the rule: *Multiply the cosine of angle* **To find Normal Pitch.** *of spiral by the circular pitch, and the product will be the normal pitch.* One-half the normal pitch is the proper thickness of cutter at the pitch line.

If the normal pitch and the angle are known *Divide the normal pitch by the cosine of the angle and the quotient will be the linear pitch.*

This may be required in a case of a spiral pinion running in a rack. The perpendicular to the side of the rack is taken as the line from which to calculate angle of teeth. That is, this line would correspond to the axial line in spiral gears. This considers a rack as a gear of infinitely long radius; page 12. If the condition required gives the angle of axis of gear and the side of the rack, we subtract the given angle from 90 degrees and base our caculations upon the remainder, which is *complement* of the given angle.

The addendum and working depth of tooth should correspond to the *normal pitch*, and not to the circular pitch. Thus, if the normal pitch is 12 diametral, the addendum should be $\frac{1}{12}''$, the thickness .1309", and so on. The diameter of pitch circle of a spiral gear is calculated from the *diametral* pitch. Thus a gear of 30 teeth 10 P would be 3" pitch diameter.

But if the normal pitch is 12 diametral pitch, the blank will be $3\frac{2}{12}''$ diameter instead of $3\frac{2}{10}''$.

Normal Pitch varies. It is evident that the normal pitch varies with the angle of spiral. The cutter should be for the normal pitch. In designing spiral gears, it is well to first look over list of cutters on hand, and see if there are cutters to which the gears can be made to conform. This may avoid the necessity of getting a new cutter, or of changing both drawing and gears after they are under way. To do this, the problem is worked the reverse of the foregoing; that is:

First calculate to the next finer pitch cutter than would be required for the diametral pitch. *To make Angle of Spiral conform to Cutters given.*

Let us take, for example, a gear 10 pitch and 30 teeth spiral. Let the next finer cutter be for 12 pitch gears. The first thing is to find the angle that will make the normal pitch .2618″, when the circular pitch is .3142″. See table of tooth parts. This means (Fig. 63) that the line A D C will be .3142″ when A E B is .2618″. Dividing .2618″ by .3142″ (see Chapter IV.), we obtain the cosine of the angle C A B, which is also the angle of the spiral, $\frac{.2618}{.3142}=.833$.

The same quotient comes by dividing 10 by 12. $\frac{10}{12}=.833+$. Looking in the table, we find the angle corresponding to the cosine .833 is 33° 30′. We now want to find the pitch of spiral that will give angle of 33½° on the pitch surface of the wheel, 3″ diameter. Dividing the circumference by the tangent of angle, we obtain the pitch of spiral (see Chapter V.) The circumference is 9.4248″. The tangent of 33° 30′ is .66188, $\frac{9.4248}{.66188}=14.23$; and we have for our spiral 14.23″ lead.

When the machine is not arranged for the exact pitch of spiral wanted, it is generally well enough to take the next nearest spiral. A half of an inch more or less in a spiral 10″ pitch or more would hardly be noticed in angle of teeth. It is generally better to take the next longer spiral and cut enough deeper to bring center distances right. When two gears of the same size are in mesh with their axes parallel, a change of angle of teeth or spiral makes no difference in the correct meshing of the teeth. *When exact Pitch cannot be cut.*

But when gears of different size are in mesh, due regard must be had to the spirals being in pitch, pro- *Spiral Gears of Different Sizes to Mesh.*

Shape of Cutter.

portional to their angular velocities (see Chapter V.)
We come now to the curvature of cutters for spiral
gears; that is, their shape as to whether a cutter is
made to cut 12 teeth or 100 teeth. A cutter that is right,
to cut a spur gear 3″ diameter, may not be right for a
spiral gear 3″ diameter. To find the curvature of
cutter, fit a templet to the blank along the line of the
normal helix, as A E B, letting the templet reach over
about two or three normal pitches. The curvature of
this templet will be nearer a straight line than an arc
of the addendum circle. Now find the diameter of a
circle that will fit this templet, and consider this circle
as the addendum circle of a gear for which we are to
select a cutter, reckoning the gear as of a pitch the
same as the normal pitch.

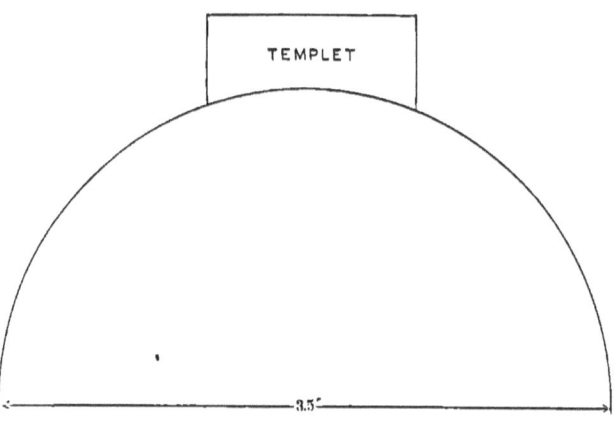

Fig. 64.

Thus, in Fig. 64, suppose the templet fits a circle
3½″ diameter, if the normal pitch is 12 to inch, diametral, the cutter required is for 12 P and 40 teeth.
The curvature of the templet will not be quite circular,
but is sufficiently near for practical purposes. Strictly,
a flat templet cannot be made to coincide with the
normal helix for any distance whatever, but any greater
refinement than we have suggested can hardly be
carried out in a workshop.

This applies more to an end cutter, for a disk cutter may have the right shape for a tooth space and still round off the teeth too much on account of the warped nature of the teeth.

The difference between normal pitch and linear or circular pitch is plainly seen in Figs 58 and 59.

The rack D D, Fig. 58, is of regular form, the depth of teeth being $\frac{11}{16}$ of the circular pitch, nearly (.6866 of the pitch, accurately). If a section of a tooth in either of the gears be made square across the tooth, that is a normal section, the depth of the tooth will have the same relation to the thickness of the tooth as in the rack just named.

But the teeth of spiral gears, looking at them upon the side of the gears, are thicker in proportion to their depth, as in Fig. 59. This difference is seen between the teeth of the two racks D D and E E, Fig. 58. In the rack D D we have 20 teeth, while in the rack E E we have but 14 teeth; yet each rack will run with each of the spiral gears A, B or C, Fig. 59, but at different angles.

The teeth of one rack will accurately fit the teeth of the other rack face to face, but the sides of one rack will then be at an angle of 45° with the sides of the other rack. At F is a guide for holding a rack in mesh with a gear.

The reason the racks will each run with either of the three gears is because all the gears and racks have the same normal pitch. When the spiral gears are to run together they must both have the same normal pitch. Hence two spiral gears may run correctly together though the circular pitch of one gear is not like the circular pitch of the other gear.

CHAPTER VII.
SCREW GEARS AND SPIRAL GEARS—GENERAL REMARKS.

Working of Spiral Gears. The working of spiral gears is generally smoother than spur gears. A tooth does not strike along its whole face or length at once. Tooth contact first takes place at one side of the gear, passes across the face and ceases at the other side of the gear. This action tends to cover defects in shape of teeth and the adjustment of centers.

Since the invention of machines for producing accurate epicyloidal and involute curves, it has not so often been found necessary to resort to spiral gears for smoothness of action. A greater range can be had in the adjustment of centers in spiral gears than in spur gears. The angle of the teeth should be enough, so that one pair of teeth will not part contact at one side of the gears until the next pair of teeth have met on the other side of the gears. When this is done the gears will be in mesh so long as the circumferences of their addendum circles intersect each other. This is sometimes necessary in roll gears.

Relative to spur and bevel gears in Part I., Chapter XII., it was stated that all gears finally wore themselves out of shape and might become noisy. Spiral gears may be worn out of shape, but the smoothness of action can hardly be impaired so long as there are any teeth left. For every quantity of wear, of course, there will be an equal quantity of backlash, so that if gears have to be reversed the lost motion in spiral gears will be as much as in any gears, and may be *End Pressure upon Shafts of Spiral Gears.* more if there is end play of the shafts. In spiral gears there is end pressure upon the shafts, because of the screw-like action of the teeth. This end pressure is sometimes balanced by putting two gears upon each shaft, one of right and one of left hand spiral.

The same result is obtained in solid cast gears by making the pattern in two parts—one right and one left-hand spiral. Such gears are colloquially called "herring-bone gears."

In an internal spiral gear and its pinion, the spirals of both wheels are either right-handed or left-handed. Such a combination would hardly be a mercantile product, although interesting as mechanical feat.

In screw or worm-gears the axes are generally at right angles, or nearly so. The distinctive features of screw gearing may be stated as follows:

The relative angular velocities do not depend upon the diameters of pitch-cylinders, as in Chapter I., Part I. Thus the worm in Chapter XI., Fig. 35, can be any diameter—one inch or ten inches—without affecting the velocity of the worm-wheel. Conversely if the axes are not parallel we can have a pair of spiral or screw gears of the same diameter, but of different numbers of teeth. The direction in which a worm-wheel turns depends upon whether the worm has a right-hand or left-hand thread. When angles of axes of worm and worm-wheel are oblique, there is a practical limit to the directional relation of the worm-wheel. The rotation of the worm-wheel is made by the end movement of the worm-thread. *(Distinctive features of Screw Gearing.)*

The term worm and worm-wheel, or worm-gearing, is applied to cases where the worms are cut in a lathe.

If we let two cylinders touch each other, their axes be at right angles, the rotation of one cylinder will have no tendency to turn the other cylinder, as in Chapter I., Part I.

We can now see why worms and worm-wheels wear out faster than other gearing. The length of worm-thread, equal to more than the entire circumference of worm, comes in sliding contact with each tooth of the wheel during one turn of the wheel. *(Why Wheels Worm wear so fast.)*

The angle of a worm-thread can be calculated the same as the angle of teeth of spiral gear.

CHAPTER VIII.

CONTINUED FRACTIONS—SOME APPLICATIONS IN MACHINE CONSTRUCTION.

Definition of a Continued Fraction. A continued fraction is one which has unity for its numerator, and for its denominator an entire number plus a fraction, which fraction has also unity for its numerator, and for its denominator an entire number plus a fraction, and thus in order.

The expression, $\dfrac{1}{4+\dfrac{1}{3+\dfrac{1}{5}}}$ is called a continued fraction. By the use of continued fractions, we are enabled to find a fraction expressed in smaller numbers, that, for practical purposes, may be sufficiently near in value to another fraction expressed in large numbers. If we were required to cut a worm that would mesh with a gear 4 diametral pitch (4 P.), in a lathe having 3 to 1-inch linear leading screw, we might, without continued fractions, have trouble in finding change gears, because the circular pitch corresponding to 4 diametral pitch is expressed in large numbers:

Practical use of Continued Fractions.

$4\text{ P}=\dfrac{7854}{10000}\text{ P}'$.

This example will be considered farther on. For illustration, we will take a simpler example.

What fraction expressed in smaller numbers is nearest in value to $\dfrac{29}{145}$? Dividing the numerator and the denominator of a fraction by the same number does not change the value of the fraction. Dividing both terms of $\dfrac{29}{145}$ by 29, we have $\dfrac{1}{5\frac{1}{29}}$, or, what is the same thing expressed as a continued fraction, $\dfrac{1}{5+\dfrac{1}{29}}$. The continued fraction $\dfrac{1}{5+\dfrac{1}{29}}$ is exactly equal to $\dfrac{29}{145}$. If now, we reject the $\dfrac{1}{29}$, the fraction $\dfrac{1}{5}$ will be larger than $\dfrac{1}{5+\dfrac{1}{29}}$, because the denominator has been diminished, 5 being less than $5\frac{1}{29}$. $\dfrac{1}{5}$ is something near $\dfrac{29}{145}$ expressed in smaller numbers than 29 for a

Example in Continued Fractions.

numerator and 146 for a denominator. Reducing $\frac{1}{5}$ and $\frac{29}{146}$ to a common denominator, we have $\frac{1}{5}=\frac{146}{730}$ and $\frac{29}{146}=\frac{145}{730}$. Subtracting one from the other, we have $\frac{1}{730}$, which is the difference between $\frac{1}{5}$ and $\frac{29}{146}$. Thus, in thinking of $\frac{29}{146}$ as $\frac{1}{5}$, we have a pretty fair idea of its value.

There are fourteen fractions with terms smaller than 29 and 146, which are nearer $\frac{29}{146}$ than $\frac{1}{5}$ is, such as $\frac{1}{6}, \frac{2}{11}$ and so on to $\frac{28}{141}$. In this case by continued fractions we obtain only one approximation, namely $\frac{1}{5}$, and any other approximations, as $\frac{1}{6}, \frac{2}{11}$, &c., we find by trial. It will be noted that all these approximations are greater in value than $\frac{29}{146}$. There are cases, however, in which we can, by continued fractions, obtain approximations both greater and less than the required fraction, and these will be the nearest possible approximations that there can be in smaller terms than the given fraction.

In the French metric system, a millimetre is equal to .03937 inch; what fraction in smaller terms expresses .03937" nearly? .03937, in a vulgar fraction, is $\frac{3937}{100000}$. Dividing both numerator and denominator by 3937, we have $\frac{1}{25\frac{1575}{3937}}$. Rejecting from the denominator of the new fraction, $\frac{1575}{3937}$, the fraction $\frac{1}{25}$ gives us a pretty good idea of the value of .03937". If in the expression, $\frac{1}{25+\frac{1575}{3937}}$, we divide both terms of the fraction $\frac{1575}{3937}$ by 1575, the value will not be changed. Performing the division, we have
$$\cfrac{1}{25 + \cfrac{1}{2 + \frac{787}{1575}}}.$$

We can now divide both terms of $\frac{787}{1575}$ by 787, without changing its value, and then substitute the new fraction for $\frac{787}{1575}$ in the continued fraction.

Dividing again, and substituting, we have:
$$\cfrac{1}{25 + \cfrac{1}{2 + \cfrac{1}{2 + \frac{1}{787}}}}$$

as the continued fraction that is exactly equal to .03937.

In performing the divisions, the work stands thus:

```
3937) 100000 (25
      7874
      ─────
      21260
      19685
      ─────
      1575) 3937 (2
            3150
            ────
            787) 1575 (2
                 1574
                 ────
                 1) 787 (787
                    787
                    ───
                     0
```

That is, dividing the last divisor by the last remainder, as in finding the greatest common divisor. The quotients become the denominators of the continued fraction, with unity for numerators. The denominators 25, 2, and so on, are called incomplete quotients, since they are only the entire parts of each quotient. The first expression in the continued fraction is $\frac{1}{25}$ or .04—a little larger than .03937. If, now, we take $\frac{1}{25+\frac{1}{2}}$, we shall come still nearer .03937. The expression $\frac{1}{25+\frac{1}{2}}$ is merely stating that 1 is to be divided by $25\frac{1}{2}$. To divide, we first reduce $25\frac{1}{2}$ to an improper fraction, $\frac{51}{2}$, and the expression becomes $\frac{1}{\frac{51}{2}}$, or one divided by $\frac{51}{2}$. To divide by a fraction, "Invert the divisor, and proceed as in multiplication." We then have $\frac{2}{51}$ as the next nearest fraction to .03937. $\frac{2}{51}=.0392+$, which is smaller than .03937. To get still nearer, we take in the next part of the continued fraction, and have

$$\frac{1}{25+\frac{1}{2+\frac{1}{2}}}$$

We can bring the value of this expression into a fraction, with only one number for its numerator and one number for its denominator, by performing the operations indicated, step by step, commencing at the last part of the continued fraction. Thus, $2+\frac{1}{2}$, or $2\frac{1}{2}$, is equal to $\frac{5}{2}$. Stopping here, the continued fraction would become

$$\frac{1}{25+\frac{1}{\frac{5}{2}}}$$

Now, $\frac{1}{\frac{5}{2}}$ equals $\frac{2}{5}$, and we have $\frac{1}{25+\frac{2}{5}}$. $25\frac{2}{5}$ equals $\frac{127}{5}$; substituting again, we have $\frac{1}{\frac{127}{5}}$. Dividing 1 by $\frac{127}{5}$, we have $\frac{5}{127}$. $\frac{5}{127}$ is the nearest fraction to

.03937, unless we reduce the whole continued fraction
$$\cfrac{1}{25+\cfrac{1}{2+\cfrac{1}{2+\frac{1}{787}}}},$$ which would give us back the .03937 itself.
$\frac{6}{127}=.03937007$, which is only $\frac{7}{1000000000}$ larger .03937. It is not often that an approximation will come so near as this.

This ratio, 5 to 127, is used in cutting millimeter thread screws. If the leading screw of the lathe is 1 to one inch, the change gears will have the ratio of 5 to 127; if 8 to one inch, the ratio will be 8 times as large, or 40 to 127; so that with leading screw 8 to inch, and change gears 40 and 127, we can cut millimeter threads near enough for practical purposes. **Practical use of the foregoing Example.**

The foregoing operations are more tedious in description than in use. The steps have been carefully noted, so that the reason for each step can be seen from rules of common arithmetic, the operations being merely reducing complex fractions. The reductions, $\frac{1}{25}$, $\frac{2}{51}$, $\frac{5}{127}$, etc., are called *convergents*, because they come nearer and nearer to the required .03937. The operations can be shortened as follows:

Let us find the fractions converging towards .7854", **Example.** the circular pitch of 4 diametral pitch, $.7854 = \frac{7854}{10000}$; reducing to lowest terms, we have $\frac{3927}{5000}$. Applying the operation for the greatest common divisor:

```
   3927) 5000 (1
         3927
         1073) 3927 (3
               3219
               708) 1073 (1
                    708
                    365) 708 (1
                         365
                         343) 365 (1
                              343
                              22) 343 (15
                                  22
                                  123
                                  110
                                  13) 22 (1
                                      13
                                      9) 13 (1
                                         9
                                         4) 9 (2
                                            8
                                            1) 4 (4
                                               4
                                               0
```

Bringing the various incomplete quotients as denominators in a continued fraction as before, we have:

$$\cfrac{1}{1+\cfrac{1}{3+\cfrac{1}{1+\cfrac{1}{1+\cfrac{1}{1+\cfrac{1}{15+\cfrac{1}{1+\cfrac{1}{1+\cfrac{1}{2+\frac{1}{4}}}}}}}}}}$$

Now arrange each partial quotient in a line, thus:

1	3	1	1	1	15	1	1	2	4
1	$\tfrac{3}{4}$	$\tfrac{4}{5}$	$\tfrac{7}{9}$	$\tfrac{11}{14}$	$\tfrac{172}{219}$	$\tfrac{183}{233}$	$\tfrac{355}{452}$	$\tfrac{893}{1137}$	$\tfrac{3927}{5000}$

Now place under the first incomplete quotient the first reduction or convergent $\tfrac{1}{1}$, which, of course, is 1; put under the next partial quotient the next reduction or convergent $\tfrac{1}{1+\tfrac{1}{3}}$ or $\tfrac{1}{1\tfrac{1}{3}}$, which becomes $\tfrac{3}{4}$.

1 is larger than .7854, and $\tfrac{3}{4}$ is less than .7854.

Having made two reductions, as previously shown, we can shorten the operations by the following rule for next convergents: *Multiply the numerator of the convergent just found by the denominator of the next term of the continued fraction, or the next incomplete quotient, and add to the product the numerator of the preceding convergent; the sum will be the numerator of the next convergent.*

Proceed in the same way for the denominator, that is multiply the denominator of the convergent just found by the next incomplete quotient and add to the product the denominator of the preceding convergent; the sum will be the denominator of the next convergent. Continue until the last convergent is the original fraction. Under each incomplete quotient or denominator from the continued fraction arranged in line, will be seen the corresponding convergent or reduction. The convergent $\tfrac{11}{14}$ is the one commonly used in cutting racks 4 P. This is the same as calling the circumference of a circle 22-7 when the diameter is one (1); this is also the common ratio for cutting any rack. The equivalent decimal to $\tfrac{11}{14}$ is .7857×, being about $\tfrac{3}{10000}$ large. In three settings for rack teeth, this error would amount to about .001″

For a worm, this corresponds to $\tfrac{11}{14}$ threads to 1″; now, with a leading screw of lathe 3 to 1″, we would want gears on the spindle and screw in a ratio of 33 to 14.

Hence, a gear on the spindle with 66 teeth, and a gear on the 3 thread screw of 28 teeth, would enable us to cut a worm to fit a 4 P gear.

CHAPTER IX.

ANGLE OF PRESSURE.

In Fig. 47, let A be any flat disk lying upon a horizontal plane. Take any piece, B, with a square end, $a\,b$. Press against A with the piece B in the direction of the arrow.

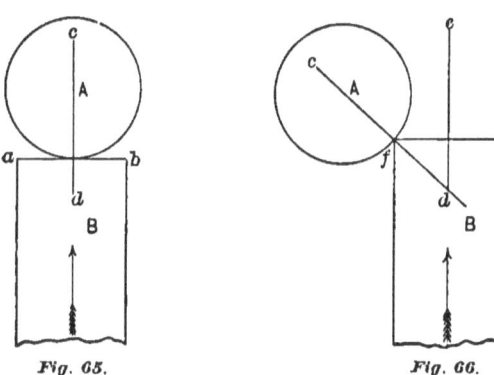

Fig. 65.   *Fig. 66.*

It is evident A will tend to move directly ahead of B in the normal line $c\,d$. Now (Fig. 66) let the piece B, at one corner f, touch the piece A. Move the piece B along the line $d\,e$, in the direction of the arrow.

It is evident that A will not now tend to move in the line $d\,e$, but will tend to move in the direction of the normal $c\,d$. When one piece, not attached, presses against another, the tendency to move the second piece is in the direction of the normal, at the point of contact. This normal is called the *line of pressure*. Line of Pressure. The angle that this line makes with the path of the impelling piece, is called the *angle of pressure*.

In Part I., Chapter IV., the lines B A and B A' are called lines of pressure. This means that if the gear drives the rack, the *tendency* to move the rack is not in the direction of pitch line of rack, but either in the direction B A or B A', as we turn the wheel to the left or to the right.

The same law holds if the rack is moved in the direction of the pitch line; the *tendency* to move the wheel is not directly tangent to the pitch circle, as if driven by a belt, but in the direction of the line of pressure. Of course the rack and wheel *do* move in the paths prescribed by their connections with the framework, the wheel turning about its axis and the rack moving along its ways. This pressure, not in a direct path of the moving piece, causes extra friction in all toothed gearing that cannot well be avoided.

Although this pressure works out by the diagram, as we have shown, yet, in the actual gears, it is not at all certain that they will follow the law as stated, because of the friction of teeth among themselves. If the driver in a train of gears has no bearing upon its tooth-flank, we apprehend there will be but little tendency to press the shafts apart.

Arc of Action. The arc through which a wheel passes while one of its teeth is in contact is called the *arc of action*.

Base of System of Interchangeable Gears. Until within a few years, the base of a system of double-curve interchangeable gears was 12 teeth. It is now 15 teeth in the best practice (see Chapter VII., Part I.)

The reason for this change was: the base, 15 teeth, gives less angle of pressure and longer arc of contact, and hence longer lifetime of gears.

CHAPTER X.

INTERNAL GEARS.

In Part I., Chapter VIII., it was stated that the space of an internal gear is the same as the tooth of a spur gear. This applies to involute or single-curve gears as well as to double-curve gears.

The sides of teeth in involute internal gears will be hollowing. It, however, has been customary to cut internal gears with spur gear-cutters, a No. 1 cutter generally being used. This makes the teeth sides convex. Special cutters should be made for coarse pitch double-curve gears. In designing internal gears, it is sometimes necessary to depart from the system with 15-tooth base, so as to have the pinion differ from the wheel by less than 15 teeth. The rules given in Part I., Chapters VII. and VIII., will apply in making gears on any base besides 15 teeth. If the base is low-numbered and the pinion is small, it may be necessary to resort to the method given at the end of Chapter VII., because the teeth may be too much rounded at the points by following the approximate rules. The base must be as small as the *difference* between the internal gear and its pinion. The base can be smaller if desired. {Special Cutters for coarse Pitch.} {Base for Internal Gear Teeth.}

Let it be required to make an internal gear, and pinion 24 and 18 teeth, 3 P. Here the base cannot be more than 6 teeth.

In Fig. 67 the base is 6 teeth. The arcs A K and O k, drawn about T, have a radius equal to the radius of the pitch circle of a 6-tooth gear, 3 P, instead of a 15-tooth gear, as in Chapter VIII., Part I.

The *outline* of teeth of both gears and pinion is made similar to the gear in Chapter VIII. The same {Description of Fig. 67.}

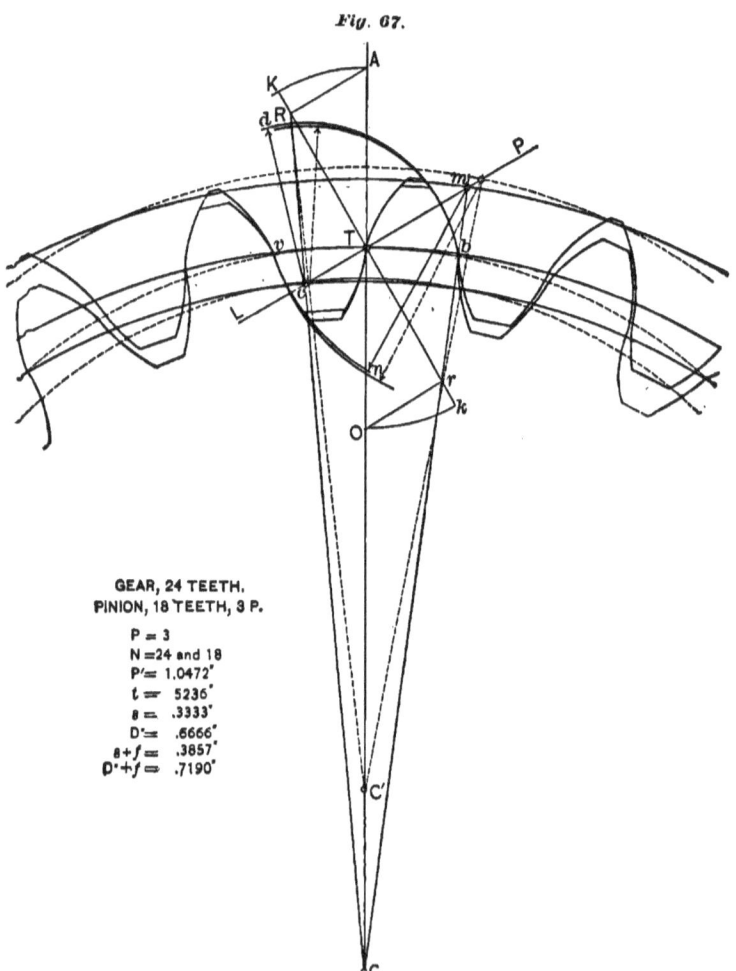

Fig. 67.

GEAR, 24 TEETH.
PINION, 18 TEETH, 3 P.

$P = 3$
$N = 24$ and 18
$P' = 1.0472''$
$t = .5236''$
$s = .3333''$
$D' = .6666''$
$s+f = .3857''$
$D'+f = .7190''$

INTERNAL GEAR AND PINION IN MESH.

letters refer to similar parts. The clearance circle is, however, drawn on the *outside* for the internal gear. As before stated, the spaces of a spur wheel become the *teeth* of an internal wheel. The teeth of internal gears require but little for fillets at the roots; they are generally strong enough without fillets. The teeth of the pinion are also similar to the gear in Chapter VIII., substituting 6-tooth for 15-tooth base. To avoid confusion, it is well to make a complete sketch of one gear before making the other. The arc of action is longer in internal gears than in external gears. This property sometimes makes it necessary to give less fillets than in external gears.

In Fig. 67 the angle K T A is 30° instead of 12°, as in Fig. 12. This brings the line of pressure L P at an angle of 60° with the radius C T, instead of 78°. A system of spur gears could be made upon this 6-tooth base. These gears would interchange, but no gear of this 6-tooth system would mesh with a double-curve gear made upon the 15-tooth system in Part 1.

CHAPTER XI.

STRENGTH OF GEARING.

We have been unable to derive from our own experience, any definite rule on this subject, but would refer those interested to "Kent's Mechanical Engineers' Pocket Book," where a good treatment of the subject can be found.

We give a few examples of average breaking strain of our Combination Gears, as determined by dynamometer, the pressure being measured at the pitch line. These gears are of cast iron, with cut teeth.

DIAMETRAL PITCH.	FACE.	No. TEETH.	REVOLUTIONS PER MINUTE.	PRESSURE AT PITCH LINE.
10	1 1-16	110	27	1060
8	1 1-4	72	40	1460
6	1 9-16	72	27	2220
5	1 7-8	90	18	2470

These are the actual pressures for the particular widths given.

If we take a safe pressure at 1-3 of the foregoing breaking strain, we shall have for

10 Pitch 353 1-3 Lbs. at the Pitch Line.
8 " 486 2-3 " "
6 " 740 " "
5 " 823 1-3 " "

The width of the face of a gear is in good proportion when it is $2\frac{1}{2}$ times the circular pitch. Brown & Sharpe's rule is, width $= \frac{8}{P} + .25''$

TABLE OF DECIMAL EQUIVALENTS

OF MILLIMETERS AND FRACTIONS OF MILLIMETERS.

mm.	Inches.	mm.	Inches.	mm.	Inches.
$\frac{1}{60}=$	.00079	$\frac{26}{60}=$	.02047	2=	.07874
$\frac{2}{60}=$	.00157	$\frac{27}{60}=$	.02126	3=	.11811
$\frac{3}{60}=$	.00236	$\frac{28}{60}=$	.02205	4=	.15748
$\frac{4}{60}=$	.00315	$\frac{29}{60}=$	.02283	5=	.19685
$\frac{5}{60}=$	.00394	$\frac{30}{60}=$	.02362	6=	.23622
$\frac{6}{60}=$	.00472	$\frac{31}{60}=$	.02441	7=	.27559
$\frac{7}{60}=$	.00551	$\frac{32}{60}=$	.02520	8=	.31496
$\frac{8}{60}=$	.00630	$\frac{33}{60}=$	.02598	9=	.35433
$\frac{9}{60}=$	.00709	$\frac{34}{60}=$	.02677	10=	.39370
$\frac{10}{60}=$	.00787	$\frac{35}{60}=$	.02756	11=	.43307
$\frac{11}{60}=$	.00866	$\frac{36}{60}=$	.02835	12=	.47244
$\frac{12}{60}=$	.00945	$\frac{37}{60}=$	.02913	13=	.51181
$\frac{13}{60}=$	.01024	$\frac{38}{60}=$	.02992	14=	.55118
$\frac{14}{60}=$	.01102	$\frac{39}{60}=$	.03071	15=	.59055
$\frac{15}{60}=$	.01181	$\frac{40}{60}=$	.03150	16=	.62992
$\frac{16}{60}=$	.01260	$\frac{41}{60}=$	.03228	17=	.66929
$\frac{17}{60}=$	.01339	$\frac{42}{60}=$	.03307	18=	.70866
$\frac{18}{60}=$	.01417	$\frac{43}{60}=$	.03386	19=	.74803
$\frac{19}{60}=$	.01496	$\frac{44}{60}=$	.03465	20=	.78740
$\frac{20}{60}=$	.01575	$\frac{45}{60}=$	.03543	21=	.82677
$\frac{21}{60}=$	.01654	$\frac{46}{60}=$	.03622	22=	.86614
$\frac{22}{60}=$	.01732	$\frac{47}{60}=$	.03701	23=	.90551
$\frac{23}{60}=$	.01811	$\frac{48}{60}=$	.03780	24=	.94488
$\frac{24}{60}=$	.01890	$\frac{49}{60}=$	.03858	25=	.98425
$\frac{25}{60}=$	.01969	1=	.03937	26=	1.02362

10 mm. = 1 Centimeter = 0.3937 inches.
10 cm. = 1 Decimeter = 3.937 "
10 dm. = 1 Meter = 39.37 "
25.4 mm. = 1 English Inch.

NATURAL SINE.

Deg.	0′	10′	20′	30′	40′	50′	60′	
0	.00000	.00291	.00581	.00872	.01163	.01454	.01745	89
1	.01745	.02036	.02326	.02617	.02908	.03199	.03489	88
2	.03489	.03780	.04071	.04361	.04652	.04943	.05233	87
3	.05233	.05524	.05814	.06104	.06395	.06685	.06975	86
4	.06975	.07265	.07555	.07845	.08155	.08425	.08715	85
5	.08715	.09005	.09295	.09584	.09874	.10163	.10452	84
6	.10452	.10742	.11031	.11320	.11609	.11898	.12186	83
7	.12186	.12475	.12764	.13052	.13341	.13629	.13917	82
8	.13917	.14205	.14493	.14780	.15068	.15356	.15643	81
9	.15643	.15930	.16217	.16504	.16791	.17078	.17364	80
10	.17364	.17651	.17937	.18223	.18509	.18795	.19080	79
11	.19080	.19366	.19651	.19936	.20221	.20506	.20791	78
12	.20791	.21075	.21359	.21644	.21927	.22211	.22495	77
13	.22495	.22778	.23061	.23344	.23627	.23909	.24192	76
14	.24192	.24474	.24756	.25038	.25319	.25600	.25881	75
15	.25881	.26162	.26443	.26723	.27004	.27284	.27563	74
16	.27563	.27843	.28122	.28401	.28680	.28958	.29237	73
17	.29237	.29515	.29793	.30070	.30347	.30624	.30901	72
18	.30901	.31178	.31454	.31730	.32006	.32281	.32556	71
19	.32556	.32831	.33106	.33380	.33654	.33928	.34202	70
20	.34202	.34475	.34748	.35020	.35293	.35565	.35836	69
21	.35836	.36108	.36379	.36650	.36920	.37190	.37460	68
22	.37460	.37730	.37999	.38268	.38536	.38805	.39073	67
23	.39073	.39340	.39607	.39874	.40141	.40407	.40673	66
24	.40673	.40939	.41204	.41469	.41733	.41998	.42261	65
25	.42261	.42525	.42788	.43051	.43313	.43575	.43837	64
26	.43837	.44098	.44359	.44619	.44879	.45139	.45399	63
27	.45399	.45658	.45916	.46174	.46432	.46690	.46947	62
28	.46947	.47203	.47460	.47715	.47971	.48226	.48481	61
29	.48481	.48735	.48989	.49242	.49495	.49747	.50000	60
30	.50000	.50251	.50503	.50753	.51004	.51254	.51503	59
31	.51503	.51752	.52001	.52249	.52497	.52745	.52991	58
32	.52991	.53238	.53484	.53730	.53975	.54219	.54463	57
33	.54463	.54707	.54950	.55193	.55436	.55677	.55919	56
34	.55919	.56160	.56400	.56640	.56880	.57119	.57357	55
35	.57357	.57595	.57833	.58070	.58306	.58542	.58778	54
36	.58778	.59013	.59249	.59482	.59715	.59948	.60181	53
37	.60181	.60413	.60645	.60876	.61106	.61336	.61566	52
38	.61566	.61795	.62023	.62251	.62478	.62705	.62932	51
39	.62932	.63157	.63383	.63607	.63832	.64055	.64278	50
40	.64278	.64501	.64723	.64944	.65165	.65386	.65605	49
41	.65605	.65825	.66043	.66262	.66479	.66696	.66913	48
42	.66913	.67128	.67344	.67559	.67773	.67986	.68199	47
43	.68199	.68412	.68624	.68835	.69046	.69256	.69465	46
44	.69465	.69674	.69883	.70090	.70298	.70504	.70710	45
	60′	50′	40′	30′	20′	10′	0′	Deg.

NATURAL COSINE.

PROVIDENCE, R. I. 145

NATURAL SINE.

Deg.	0'	10'	20'	30'	40'	50'	60'	
45	.70710	.70916	.71120	.71325	.71528	.71731	.71934	44
46	.71934	.72135	.72336	.72537	.72737	.72936	.73135	43
47	.73135	.73333	.73530	.73727	.73923	.74119	.74314	42
48	.74314	.74508	.74702	.74895	.75088	.75279	.75471	41
49	.75471	.75661	.75851	.76040	.76229	.76417	.76604	40
50	.76604	.76791	.76977	.77162	.77347	.77531	.77714	39
51	.77714	.77897	.78079	.78260	.78441	.78621	.78801	38
52	.78801	.78979	.79157	.79335	.79512	.79688	.79863	37
53	.79863	.80038	.80212	.80385	.80558	.80730	.80901	36
54	.80901	.81072	.81242	.81411	.81580	.81748	.81915	35
55	.81915	.82081	.82247	.82412	.82577	.82740	.82903	34
56	.82903	.83066	.83227	.83388	.83548	.83708	.83867	33
57	.83867	.84025	.84182	.84339	.84495	.84650	.84804	32
58	.84804	.84958	.85111	.85264	.85415	.85566	.85716	31
59	.85716	.85866	.86014	.86162	.86310	.86456	.86602	30
60	.86602	.86747	.86892	.87035	.87178	.87320	.87462	29
61	.87462	.87602	.87742	.87881	.88020	.88157	.88294	28
62	.88294	.88430	.88566	.88701	.88835	.88968	.89100	27
63	.89100	.89232	.89363	.89493	.89622	.89751	.89879	26
64	.89879	.90006	.90132	.90258	.90383	.90507	.90630	25
65	.90630	.90753	.90875	.90996	.91116	.91235	.91354	24
66	.91354	.91472	.91589	.91706	.91821	.91936	.92050	23
67	.92050	.92163	.92276	.92388	.92498	.92609	.92718	22
68	.92718	.92827	.92934	.93041	.93148	.93253	.93358	21
69	.93358	.93461	.93565	.93667	.93768	.93869	.93969	20
70	.93969	.94068	.94166	.94264	.94360	.94456	.94551	19
71	.94551	.94646	.94739	.94832	.94924	.95015	.95105	18
72	.95105	.95195	.95283	.95371	.95458	.95545	.95630	17
73	.95630	.95715	.95799	.95882	.95964	.96045	.96126	16
74	.96126	.96205	.96284	.96363	.96440	.96516	.96592	15
75	.96592	.96667	.96741	.96814	.96887	.96958	.97029	14
76	.97029	.97099	.97168	.97237	.97304	.97371	.97437	13
77	.97437	.97502	.97566	.97629	.97692	.97753	.97814	12
78	.97814	.97874	.97934	.97992	.98050	.98106	.98162	11
79	.98162	.98217	.98272	.98325	.98378	.98429	.98480	10
80	.98480	.98530	.98580	.98628	.98676	.98722	.98768	9
81	.98769	.98813	.98858	.98901	.98944	.98985	.99026	8
82	.99026	.99066	.99106	.99144	.99182	.99218	.99254	7
83	.99254	.99280	.99323	.99357	.99390	.99421	.99452	6
84	.99452	.99482	.99511	.99539	.99567	.99593	.99619	5
85	.99619	.99644	.99668	.99691	.99714	.99735	.99756	4
86	.99756	.99776	.99795	.99813	.99830	.99847	.99863	3
87	.99863	.99877	.99891	.99904	.99917	.99928	.99939	2
88	.99939	.99948	.99957	.99965	.99972	.99979	.99984	1
89	.99984	.99989	.99993	.99996	.99998	.99999	1.0000	0
-	60'	50'	40'	30'	20'	10'	0'	Deg.

NATURAL COSINE.

NATURAL TANGENT.

Deg.	0′	10′	20′	30′	40′	50′	60′	
0	.00000	.00290	.00581	.00872	.01163	.01454	.01745	89
1	.01745	.02036	.02327	.02618	.02909	.03200	.03492	88
2	.03492	.03783	.04074	.04366	.04657	.04949	.05240	87
3	.05240	.05532	.05824	.06116	.06408	.06700	.06992	86
4	.06992	.07285	.07577	.07870	.08163	.08455	.08748	85
5	.08748	.09042	.09335	.09628	.09922	.10216	.10510	84
6	.10510	.10804	.11099	.11393	.11688	.11983	.12278	83
7	.12278	.12573	.12869	.13165	.13461	.13757	.14054	82
8	.14054	.14350	.14647	.14945	.15243	.15540	.15838	81
9	.15838	.16136	.16435	.16734	.17033	.17332	.17632	80
10	.17632	.17932	.18233	.18533	.18834	.19136	.19438	79
11	.19438	.19740	.20042	.20345	.20648	.20951	.21255	78
12	.21255	.21559	.21864	.22169	.22474	.22780	.23086	77
13	.23086	.23393	.23700	.24007	.24315	.24624	.24932	76
14	.24932	.25242	.25551	.25861	.26172	.26483	.26794	75
15	.26794	.27106	.27419	.27732	.28046	.28360	.28674	74
16	.28074	.28989	.29305	.29621	.29938	.30255	.30573	73
17	.30573	.30891	.31210	.31529	.31850	.32170	.32492	72
18	.32492	.32813	.33136	.33459	.33783	.34107	.34432	71
19	.34432	.34758	.35084	.35411	.35739	.36067	.36397	70
20	.36397	.36726	.37057	.37388	.37720	.38053	.38386	69
21	.38386	.38720	.39055	.39391	.39727	.40064	.40402	68
22	.40402	.40741	.41080	.41421	.41762	.42104	.42447	67
23	.42447	.42791	.43135	.43481	.43827	.44174	.44522	66
24	.44522	.44871	.45221	.45572	.45924	.46277	.46630	65
25	.46630	.46985	.47341	.47697	.48055	.48413	.48778	64
26	.48773	.49138	.49495	.49858	.50221	.50586	.50952	63
27	.50952	.51319	.51687	.52056	.52427	.52798	.53170	62
28	.53170	.53544	.53919	.54295	.54672	.55051	.55430	61
29	.55430	.55811	.56193	.56577	.56961	.57347	.57735	60
30	.57735	.58123	.58513	.58904	.59297	.59690	.60086	59
31	.60086	.60482	.60880	.61280	.61680	.62083	.62486	58
32	.62486	.62892	.63298	.63707	.64116	.64528	.64940	57
33	.64940	.65355	.65771	.66188	.66607	.67028	.67450	56
34	.67450	.67874	.68300	.68728	.69157	.69588	.70020	55
35	.70020	.70455	.70891	.71329	.71769	.72210	.72654	54
36	.72654	.73099	.73546	.73996	.74447	.74900	.75355	53
37	.75355	.75812	.76271	.76732	.77195	.77661	.78128	52
38	.78128	.78598	.79069	.79543	.80019	.80497	.80978	51
39	.80978	.81461	.81946	.82433	.82923	.83415	.83910	50
40	.83910	.84406	.84906	.85408	.85912	.86419	.86928	49
41	.86928	.87440	.87955	.88473	.88992	.89515	.90040	48
42	.90040	.90568	.91099	.91633	.92160	.92709	.93251	47
43	.93251	.93796	.94345	.94896	.95450	.96008	.96568	46
44	.96568	.97132	.97699	.98269	.98843	.99419	1.0000	45
	60′	50′	40′	30′	20′	10′	0′	Deg.

NATURAL COTANGENT.

NATURAL TANGENT.

Deg.	0'	10'	20'	30'	40'	50'	60	
45	1.0000	1.0058	1.0117	1.0176	1.0235	1.0295	1.0355	44
46	1.0355	1.0415	1.0476	1.0537	1.0599	1.0661	1.0723	43
47	1.0723	1.0786	1.0849	1.0913	1.0977	1.1041	1.1106	42
48	1.1106	1.1171	1.1236	1.1302	1.1369	1.1436	1.1503	41
49	1.1503	1.1571	1.1639	1.1708	1.1777	1.1847	1.1917	40
50	1.1917	1.1988	1.2059	1.2131	1.2203	1.2275	1.2349	39
51	1.2349	1.2422	1.2496	1.2571	1.2647	1.2723	1.2799	38
52	1.2799	1.2876	1.2954	1.3032	1.3111	1.3190	1.3270	37
53	1.3270	1.3351	1.3432	1.3514	1.3596	1.3680	1.3763	36
54	1.3763	1.3818	1.3933	1.4019	1.4106	1.4193	1.4281	35
55	1.4281	1.4370	1.4459	1.4550	1.4641	1.4733	1.4825	34
56	1.4825	1.4919	1.5013	1.5108	1.5204	1.5301	1.5398	33
57	1.5398	1.5497	1.5596	1.5696	1.5798	1.5900	1.6003	32
58	1.6003	1.6107	1.6212	1.6318	1.6425	1.6533	1.6642	31
59	1.6642	1.6753	1.6864	1.6976	1.7090	1.7204	1.7320	30
60	1.7320	1.7437	1.7555	1.7674	1.7795	1.7917	1.8040	29
61	1.8040	1.8164	1.8290	1.8417	1.8546	1.8676	1.8807	28
62	1.8807	1.8940	1.9074	1.9209	1.9347	1.9485	1.9626	27
63	1.9626	1.9768	1.9911	2.0056	2.0203	2.0352	2.0503	26
64	2.0503	2.0655	2.0809	2.0965	2.1123	2.1283	2.1445	25
65	2.1445	2.1609	2.1774	2.1943	2.2113	2.2285	2.2460	24
66	2.2460	2.2637	2.2816	2.2998	2.3182	2.3369	2.3558	23
67	2.3558	2.3750	2.3944	2.4142	2.4342	2.4545	2.4750	22
68	2.4750	2.4959	2.5171	2.5386	2.5604	2.5826	2.6050	21
69	2.6050	2.6279	2.6510	2.6746	2.6985	2.7228	2.7474	20
70	2.7474	2.7725	2.7980	2.8239	2.8502	2.8770	2.9042	19
71	2.9042	2.9318	2.9600	2.9886	3.0178	3.0474	3.0776	18
72	3.0776	3.1084	3.1397	3.1715	3.2040	3.2371	3.2708	17
73	3.2708	3.3052	3.3402	3.3759	3.4123	3.4495	3.4874	16
74	3.4874	3.5260	3.5655	3.6058	3.6470	3.6890	3.7320	15
75	3.7320	3.7759	3.8208	3.8667	3.9136	3.9616	4.0107	14
76	4.0107	4.0610	4.1125	4.1653	4.2193	4.2747	4.3314	13
77	4.3314	4.3896	4.4494	4.5107	4.5736	4.6382	4.7046	12
78	4.7046	4.7728	4.8430	4.9151	4.9894	5.0058	5.1445	11
79	5.1445	5.2256	5.3092	5.3955	5.4845	5.5763	5.6712	10
80	5.6712	5.7693	5.8708	5.9757	6.0844	6.1970	6.3137	9
81	6.3137	6.4348	6.5605	6.6911	6.8269	6.9682	7.1153	8
82	7.1153	7.2687	7.4287	7.5957	7.7703	7.9530	8.1443	7
83	8.1443	8.3449	8.5555	8.7768	9.0098	9.2553	9.5143	6
84	9.5143	9.7881	10.078	10.385	10.711	11.059	11.430	5
85	11.430	11.826	12.250	12.706	13.196	13.726	14.300	4
86	14.300	14.924	15.604	16.349	17.169	18.075	19.081	3
87	19.081	20.205	21.470	22.904	24.541	26.431	28.636	2
88	28.636	31.241	34.367	38.188	42.964	49.103	57.290	1
89	57.290	68.750	85.939	114.58	171.88	343.77	∞	0
	60'	50'	40'	30'	20'	10'	0'	Deg.

NATURAL COTANGENT.

NATURAL SECANT.

Deg.	0'	10'	20'	30'	40'	50	60'	
0	1.0000	1.0000	1.0000	1.0000	1.0000	1.0001	1.0001	89
1	1.0001	1.0002	1.0002	1.0003	1.0004	1.0005	1.0006	88
2	1.0006	1.0007	1.0008	1.0009	1.0010	1.0012	1.0013	87
3	1.0013	1.0015	1.0016	1.0018	1.0020	1.0022	1.0024	86
4	1.0024	1.0026	1.0028	1.0030	1.0033	1.0035	1.0038	85
5	1.0038	1.0040	1.0043	1.0046	1.0049	1.0052	1.0055	84
6	1.0055	1.0058	1.0061	1.0064	1.0068	1.0071	1.0075	83
7	1.0075	1.0078	1.0082	1.0086	1.0090	1.0094	1.0098	82
8	1.0098	1.0102	1.0106	1.0111	1.0115	1.0120	1.0124	81
9	1.0124	1.0129	1.0134	1.0139	1.0144	1.0149	1.0154	80
10	1.0154	1.0159	1.0164	1.0170	1.0175	1.0181	1.0187	79
11	1.0187	1.0192	1.0198	1.0204	1.0210	1.0217	1.0223	78
12	1.0223	1.0229	1.0236	1.0242	1.0249	1.0256	1.0263	77
13	1.0263	1.0269	1.0277	1.0284	1.0291	1.0298	1.0306	76
14	1.0306	1.0313	1.0321	1.0329	1.0336	1.0344	1.0352	75
15	1.0352	1.0360	1.0369	1.0377	1.0385	1.0394	1.0402	74
16	1.0402	1.0411	1.0420	1.0429	1.0438	1.0447	1.0456	73
17	1.0456	1.0466	1.0475	1.0485	1.0494	1.0504	1.0514	72
18	1.0514	1.0524	1.0534	1.0544	1.0555	1.0565	1.0576	71
19	1.0576	1.0586	1.0597	1.0608	1.0619	1.0630	1.0641	70
20	1.0641	1.0653	1.0664	1.0676	1.0687	1.0699	1.0711	69
21	1.0711	1.0723	1.0735	1.0747	1.0760	1.0772	1.0785	68
22	1.0785	1.0798	1.0810	1.0823	1.0837	1.0850	1.0863	67
23	1.0863	1.0877	1.0890	1.0904	1.0918	1.0932	1.0946	66
24	1.0946	1.0960	1.0974	1.0989	1.1004	1.1018	1.1033	65
25	1.1033	1.1048	1.1063	1.1079	1.1094	1.1110	1.1126	64
26	1.1126	1.1141	1.1157	1.1174	1.1190	1.1206	1.1223	63
27	1.1223	1.1239	1.1256	1.1273	1.1290	1.1308	1.1325	62
28	1.1325	1.1343	1.1361	1.1378	1.1396	1.1415	1.1433	61
29	1.1433	1.1452	1.1470	1.1489	1.1508	1.1527	1.1547	60
30	1.1547	1.1566	1.1586	1.1605	1.1625	1.1646	1.1666	59
31	1.1666	1.1686	1.1707	1.1728	1.1749	1.1770	1.1791	58
32	1.1791	1.1813	1.1835	1.1856	1.1878	1.1901	1.1923	57
33	1.1923	1.1946	1.1969	1.1992	1.2015	1.2038	1.2062	56
34	1.2062	1.2085	1.2109	1.2134	1.2158	1.2182	1.2207	55
35	1.2207	1.2232	1.2257	1.2283	1.2308	1.2334	1.2360	54
36	1.2360	1.2386	1.2413	1.2440	1.2466	1.2494	1.2521	53
37	1.2521	1.2549	1.2576	1.2604	1.2632	1.2661	1.2690	52
38	1.2690	1.2719	1.2748	1.2777	1.2807	1.2837	1.2867	51
39	1.2867	1.2898	1.2928	1.2959	1.2990	1.3022	1.3054	50
40	1.3054	1.3086	1.3118	1.3150	1.3183	1.3216	1.3250	49
41	1.3250	1.3283	1.3317	1.3351	1.3386	1.3421	1.3456	48
42	1.3456	1.3491	1.3527	1.3563	1.3599	1.3636	1.3673	47
43	1.3673	1.3710	1.3748	1.3785	1.3824	1.3862	1.3901	46
44	1.3901	1.3940	1.3980	1.4020	1.4060	1.4101	1.4142	45
	60'	50'	40'	30'	20'	10'	0'	Deg.

NATURAL COSECANT.

NATURAL SECANT.

Deg.	0'	10'	20'	30'	40'	50'	60'	
45	1.4142	1.4188	1.4225	1.4237	1.4309	1.4352	1.4395	44
46	1.4395	1.4439	1.4483	1.4527	1.4572	1.4617	1.4662	43
47	1.4662	1.4708	1.4755	1.4801	1.4849	1.4896	1.4944	42
48	1.4944	1.4993	1.5042	1.5091	1.5141	1.5191	1.5242	41
49	1.5242	1.5293	1.5345	1.5397	1.5450	1.5503	1.5557	40
50	1.5557	1.5611	1.5666	1.5721	1.5777	1.5833	1.5890	39
51	1.5890	1.5947	1.6005	1.6063	1.6122	1.6182	1.6242	38
52	1.6242	1.6303	1.6364	1.6426	1.6489	1.6552	1.6616	37
53	1.6616	1.6680	1.6745	1.6811	1.6878	1.6945	1.7013	36
54	1.7013	1.7081	1.7150	1.7220	1.7291	1.7362	1.7434	35
55	1.7434	1.7507	1.7580	1.7655	1.7730	1.7806	1.7882	34
56	1.7882	1.7960	1.8038	1.8118	1.8198	1.8278	1.8360	33
57	1.8360	1.8443	1.8527	1.8611	1.8697	1.8783	1.8870	32
58	1.8870	1.8959	1.9048	1.9139	1.9230	1.9322	1.9416	31
59	1.9416	1.9510	1.9606	1.9703	1.9800	1.9899	2.0000	30
60	2.0000	2.0101	2.0203	2.0307	2.0412	2.0519	2.0626	29
61	2.0626	2.0735	2.0845	2.0957	2.1070	2.1184	2.1300	28
62	2.1300	2.1417	2.1536	2.1656	2.1778	2.1901	2.2026	27
63	2.2026	2.2153	2.2281	2.2411	2.2543	2.2676	2.2811	26
64	2.2811	2.2948	2.3087	2.3228	2.3370	2.3515	2.3662	25
65	2.3662	2.3810	2.3961	2.4114	2.4269	2.4426	2.4585	24
66	2.4585	2.4747	2.4911	2.5078	2.5247	2.5418	2.5593	23
67	2.5593	2.5760	2.5949	2.6131	2.6316	2.6503	2.6694	22
68	2.6694	2.6883	2.7085	2.7285	2.7488	2.7694	2.7904	21
69	2.7904	2.8117	2.8334	2.8554	2.8778	2.9006	2.9238	20
70	2.9238	2.9473	2.9713	2.9957	3.0205	3.0458	3.0715	19
71	3.0715	3.0977	3.1243	3.1515	3.1791	3.2073	3.2360	18
72	3.2360	3.2653	3.2951	3.3255	3.3564	3.3880	3.4203	17
73	3.4203	3.4531	3.4867	3.5209	3.5558	3.5915	3.6279	16
74	3.6279	3.6651	3.7031	3.7419	3.7816	3.8222	3.8637	15
75	3.8637	3.9061	3.9495	3.9939	4.0393	4.0859	4.1335	14
76	4.1335	4.1823	4.2323	4.2836	4.3362	4.3901	4.4454	13
77	4.4454	4.5021	4.5604	4.6202	4.6816	4.7448	4.8097	12
78	4.8097	4.8764	4.9451	5.0158	5.0886	5.1635	5.2408	11
79	5.2408	5.3204	5.4026	5.4874	5.5749	5.6653	5.7587	10
80	5.7587	5.8553	5.9553	6.0588	6.1660	6.2771	6.3924	9
81	6.3924	6.5120	6.6363	6.7654	6.8997	7.0396	7.1852	8
82	7.1852	7.3371	7.4957	7.6612	7.8344	8.0156	8.2055	7
83	8.2055	8.4046	8.6137	8.8336	9.0651	9.3091	9.5667	6
84	9.5667	9.8391	10.127	10.433	10.758	11.104	11.473	5
85	11.473	11.868	12.291	12.745	13.234	13.763	14.335	4
86	14.335	14.957	15.636	16.380	17.198	18.102	19.107	3
87	19.107	20.230	21.493	22.925	24.562	26.450	28.653	2
88	28.653	31.257	34.382	38.201	42.975	49.114	57.298	1
89	57.298	68.757	85.945	114.59	171.88	343.77	∞	0
	60'	50'	40'	30'	20'	10'	0'	Deg.

NATURAL COSECANT.

TABLE OF DECIMAL EQUIVALENTS

OF 8THS, 16THS, 32NDS AND 64THS OF AN INCH.

8ths.
$\frac{1}{8}=.125$
$\frac{2}{8}=.250$
$\frac{3}{8}=.375$
$\frac{4}{8}=.500$
$\frac{5}{8}=.625$
$\frac{6}{8}=.750$
$\frac{7}{8}=.875$

16ths.
$\frac{1}{16}=.0625$
$\frac{3}{16}=.1875$
$\frac{5}{16}=.3125$
$\frac{7}{16}=.4375$
$\frac{9}{16}=.5625$
$\frac{11}{16}=.6875$
$\frac{13}{16}=.8125$
$\frac{15}{16}=.9375$

32nds.
$\frac{1}{32}=.03125$
$\frac{3}{32}=.09375$
$\frac{5}{32}=.15625$
$\frac{7}{32}=.21875$

$\frac{9}{32}=.28125$
$\frac{11}{32}=.34375$
$\frac{13}{32}=.40625$
$\frac{15}{32}=.46875$
$\frac{17}{32}=.53125$
$\frac{19}{32}=.59375$
$\frac{21}{32}=.65625$
$\frac{23}{32}=.71875$
$\frac{25}{32}=.78125$
$\frac{27}{32}=.84375$
$\frac{29}{32}=.90625$
$\frac{31}{32}=.96875$

64ths.
$\frac{1}{64}=.015625$
$\frac{3}{64}=.046875$
$\frac{5}{64}=.078125$
$\frac{7}{64}=.109375$
$\frac{9}{64}=.140625$
$\frac{11}{64}=.171875$
$\frac{13}{64}=.203125$
$\frac{15}{64}=.234375$
$\frac{17}{64}=.265625$

$\frac{19}{64}=.296875$
$\frac{21}{64}=.328125$
$\frac{23}{64}=.359375$
$\frac{25}{64}=.390625$
$\frac{27}{64}=.421875$
$\frac{29}{64}=.453125$
$\frac{31}{64}=.484375$
$\frac{33}{64}=.515625$
$\frac{35}{64}=.546875$
$\frac{37}{64}=.578125$
$\frac{39}{64}=.609375$
$\frac{41}{64}=.640625$
$\frac{43}{64}=.671875$
$\frac{45}{64}=.703125$
$\frac{47}{64}=.734375$
$\frac{49}{64}=.765625$
$\frac{51}{64}=.796875$
$\frac{53}{64}=.828125$
$\frac{55}{64}=.859375$
$\frac{57}{64}=.890625$
$\frac{59}{64}=.921875$
$\frac{61}{64}=.953125$
$\frac{63}{64}=.984375$

INDEX.

A.
                                                                PAGE.
Abbreviations of Parts of Teeth and Gears............... 4
Addendum... 2
Angle, How to Lay Off an............................ 92, 111
" Increment... 110
" of Edge... 106
" of Face... 108
" of Pressure.. 137
" of Spiral... 117
Angular Velocity... 2
Annular Gears......................................32, 139
Arc of Action... 138

B.
Base Circle... 11
" of Epicycloidal System............................. 25
" of Internal Gears.................................. 139
Bevel Gear Blanks....................................... 34
" Cutting on B. & S. Automatic Gear Cutter..... 52
" Angles by Diagram................................ 36
" " by Calculation...................106, 110
" Form of Teeth of................................. 41
" · Whole Diameter of........................36, 108

C.
Centers, Line of.. 2
Circular Pitch.. 4
Classification of Gearing............................... 5
Clearance at Bottom of Space............................ 6
" in Pattern Gears.................................. 8
Condition of Constant Velocity Ratio.................... 2
Contact, Arc of....................................... 138
Continued Fractions................................... 130
Coppering Solution..................................... 83

INDEX.

	PAGE.
Cutters, How to Order	81
" Table of Epicycloidal	82
" " of Involute	80
" " of Speeds for	79
Cutting Bevel Gears on B. & S. Automatic Gear Cutter	52

D.

Decimal Equivalents, Tables of	143, 150
Diameter Increment	108
" of Pitch Circle	6
" Pitch	5
Diametral Pitch	17
Distance between Centers	8

E.

Elements of Gear Teeth	5
Epicycloidal Gears, with more and less than 15 Teeth	30
" " with 15 Teeth	25
" Rack	27

F.

Face, Width of Spur Gear	78
Flanks of Teeth in Low-numbered Pinions	20

G.

Gear Cutters, How to Order	81
" Patterns	8
Gearing Classified	5
Gears, Bevel	34, 41, 106
" Epicycloidal	25
" Involute	9
" Spiral	113
" Worm	62

H.

Herring-bone Gears	129

I.

Increment, Angle	110
" Diameter	108
Interchangeable Gears	24
Internal or Annular Gears	139
Involute Gears, 30 Teeth and over	9
" " with Less than 30 Teeth	20
" Rack	12

INDEX. 155

L.

	PAGE.
Limiting Numbers of Teeth in Internal Gears	32
Line of Centers	2
" of Pressure	12, 137
Linear Velocity	1

M.

Machine, B. & S., for Cutting Bevel Gears............... 52

N.

Normal... 122
" Helix 122
" Pitch.. 122

O.

Original Cylinders.. 1

P.

Pattern Gears... 8
Pitch Circle 3
" Circular or Linear................................... 4
" a Diameter... 6
" Diametral.. 17
" Normal... 122
" of Spirals... 116
Polygons, Calculations for Diameters of.................. 99

R.

Rack.. 12
" for Epicycloidal Gears............................... 27
" for Involute   "   12
" for Spiral   "   127
Relative Angular Velocity................................ 2
Rolling Contact of Pitch Circle.......................... 3

S.

Screw Gearing..113, 129
Single-Curve Teeth....................................... 9
Speed of Gear Cutters.................................... 79

Spiral Gearing.. 113
Standard Templets................................ 27
Strength of Gears.................................... 142

T.

Table of Decimal Equivalents.....................143, 150
" of Sines, etc................................. 144
" of Speeds for Gear Cutters 79
" of Tooth Parts............................ 86

V.

Velocity, Angular 2
" Linear.................................. 1
" Relative................................ 2

W.

Wear of Teeth..........'.........................78, 128
Worm Gears... 62

www.ingramcontent.com/pod-product-compliance
Lightning Source LLC
Chambersburg PA
CBHW030246170426
43202CB00009B/639